Veronika Hucke spent nearly 20 years in leadership positions in communications and brand management at leading companies before assuming global responsibility for diversity, equity and inclusion at Philips. Since 2015, she has been supporting international companies and organizations including the UN with their Diversity and Inclusion (D&I) strategies and initiatives.

How to Overcome Unconscious Bias.
Practical Advice for Leaders

The original edition was published in 2019 by Campus Verlag with the title *Fair führen*.
©2019. All rights reserved.

ISBN 9781660032013

Cover design: total italic, Thierry Wijnberg, Amsterdam/Berlin

Fonts: Minon Pro und Neue Helvetica

"Today, good leadership requires fair dealings with different people. The guidebook illuminates typical blind spots and helps ensure fair interactions."
Alberto Platz,
Head of Global Talent Acquisition & Engagement, Swarovski

"This book fills a real gap in the D&I space – speaking directly to the people who really make it happen (or not), the managers. With stories about the daily situations everyone encounters and simple, practical tips, Veronika enables the people who have day jobs in the business to understand and make real contributions to creating an inclusive environment."
Jennifer O'Lear,
Chief Diversity Officer, Merck

"A clever book and a highly recommended read on leadership. Packed with real-life examples, hands-on advice and practical tips. It is also eye-opening for experienced managers because it shows how bad leadership is connected with traditional behavioral patterns, stereotypes and unconscious biases towards strangers/others, a lack of listening to the group, a lack of awareness of the processes in one's own brain, etc. This is something that ambitious organizations can no longer afford."
Thomas Piehler,
Member of the Board of Philips GmbH
and the Employer Association Nordmetall e.V.

"An excellent book, full of the most useful insights, cases and firsthand anecdotes that are a must-read for anyone working in in diverse and cross-cultural environments. The tips at the end of each chapter are worth the read alone. The clear, lucid writing is a welcome bonus!"
Shantanu Bhattacharya,
GM Digital Learning Experience at Tata Group

"The success of most companies today is based on deep customer understanding and innovation. A diverse workforce and an inclusive environment are essential for this. Still, everyday working practices remain a challenge: the ability of organizations to articulate and to deploy systematically different managerial rituals and the adoption of individual attitudes and behaviors. That's exactly the strength of this book. It offers pragmatic recommendations for action in day-to-day situations which can be easily implemented."

Frank Waldmann,
CHRO, Rexel

"You can clearly tell that Veronika is both, an experienced senior leader and a diversity and inclusion expert with many years of internal experience. This book fills a gap. It offers practical support for all managers that value fairness and want to create an environment in which everyone thrives."

Lisa Kepinski,
Founder & Director, Inclusion Institute

"Veronika Hucke has written a compelling book for managers who are looking to lead fairly and inclusively. This book is full of tips and tricks on how to get there. An essential read for all managers keen to make a real difference!"

Elisabeth Kelan,
Professor of Leadership and Organisation,
Essex Business School, University of Essex, UK

"Veronika Hucke's book is entertaining and fun to read. It uses storytelling to depict everyday situations that we all know, and it conveys scientific knowledge to explain what is actually going on. Coupled with hands-on advice, practical tools and checklists, it's a must read for leaders, HR professionals and members of diverse management teams."
Andrea Bodstein-Walenciak,
CHRO, Kramp Group

"Are the nice guys and girls the ones who are thrown under the bus? Are teams who work across distances low-performing? Are the winners the ones with sharp elbows and a talent for exploiting others? Veronika makes a case for a triple No. In this book, you find proof for the solid advantages of playing a fair game in business. Yes, today's business world is about being competent and competitive. However, it is also about support, open-mindedness, and diversity. And last but not least, it is about giving safety, earning trust and - well, just being warm and friendly. An amazing book!"
Sylvia Loehken,
Author of "The Power of Personality: How Introverts and Extroverts Can Combine to Amazing Effect

Table of Contents

Preface 15

Why leading fairly is difficult and why it matters 17

PART 1
DAY BY DAY

Get over it! 29
How micro-inequities and micro-aggression stop us f
rom having fun at work

Covering 39
What it means when you can't be
who you are at work

Birds of a feather flock together 48
Why our existing network is rarely future-proof
and how to develop it systematically

PART 2
TEAM WORK

No one could possibly have seen that coming! 63
Why homogeneous teams and groupthink
make for worse results

You always do that exceptionally well! 73
Why delegation is often unfair and thwarts employees

Could you quickly give me a hand? 82
Why successful collaboration needs rules and how to
address conflict

PART 3
GETTING IN AND UP

I know the perfect candidate! 95
How we exclude people during the application process

He doesn't look the part! 111
Why qualification is often not the most decisive factor
for promotions

**I didn't yet have a chance
to provide feedback** 125
Why we sometimes avoid giving feedback and
how to make it work

PART 4
REMOTE, DIGITAL AND INTERNATIONAL

Out of sight, out of mind 141
Why distance impacts opportunities and how to address that

That sounds Greek to me 150
Why it is normal that others behave differently
even if it puzzles me

That's never going to work! 162
How to be successful with international teams

PART 5
WOMEN AND MEN

**I need to leave early today,
the preschoolers are putting on a play** 175
How warmth and competence impact our judgement

Don't blow your own trumpet 184
How our expectations impact our judgement

Cat fight 195
Why it matters to step up and support others

AND NOW?

Fair Leadership 207
How to create an environment in which everyone thrives

Thank you 214

Glossary 216

Bibliography 220

Notes 222

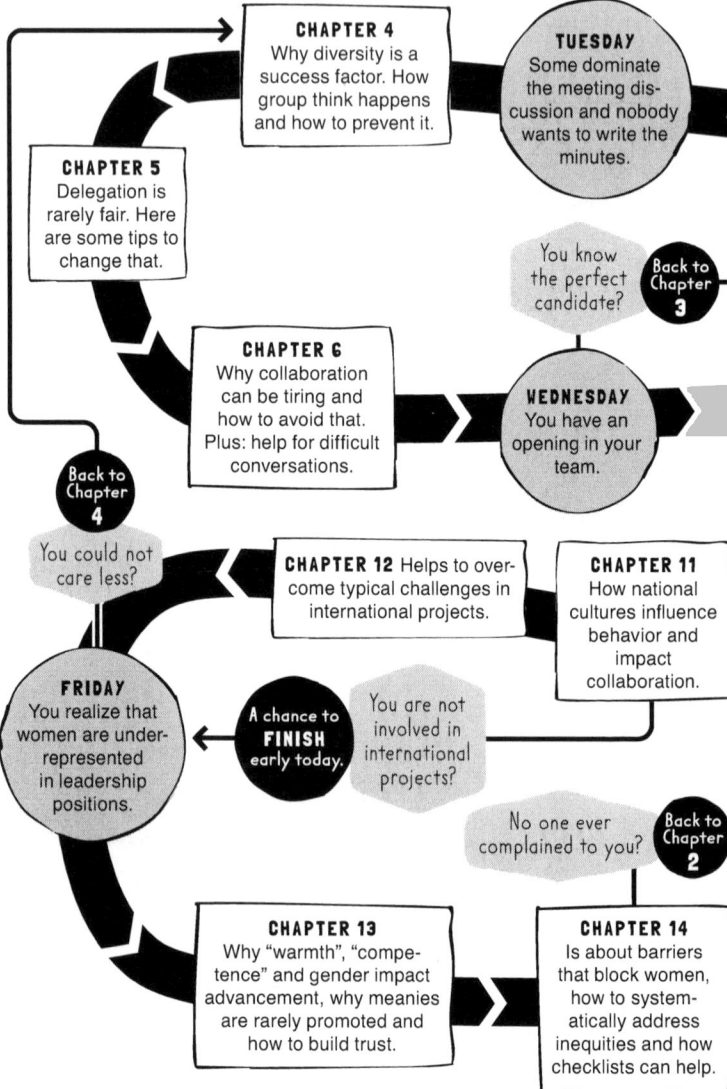

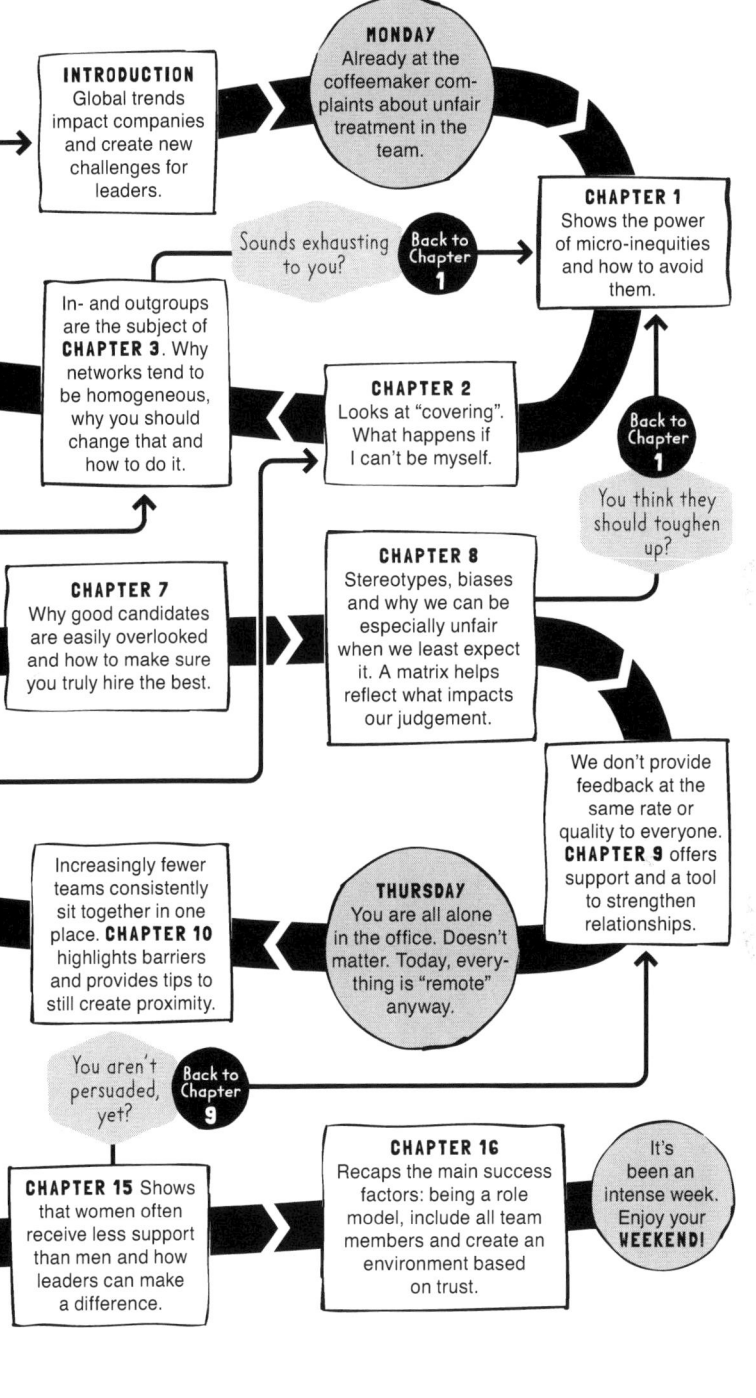

Preface

It has been said that "people don't leave companies. They leave their managers". Maybe you have been in that same position and have left a place of employment? If so, you are in good company. About half of all employees say that they have left a job due to their boss. Because fun at work and a team's success strongly depend on the manager. Do I like going to work or do I wish it was Friday already? Do I stretch myself or navigate through the day with minimum effort? Do I feel engaged and supported or simply frustrated?

Great managers possess five talents. They motivate their employees, assert themselves to overcome obstacles, create a culture of accountability, build trusting relationships and make informed, unbiased decisions for the good of their team and company.[1]

That enables them to create a fair environment. One, where people have trust and can depend on each other. Where everyone can be themselves and it is easy to admit mistakes or that one is not sure about a decision. Where one can share ideas even outside their scope of responsibility – and even mad ones. Such an environment makes it OK and even desirable to challenge each other. And that's how one gets the perfect conditions for exceptional results.

This book explores why not all teams operate like that – and what you can do to make sure that yours does.

Important terms used in this book are explained in the glossary. They are marked with → the first time they are mentioned.

Introduction
Why leading fairly is difficult and why it matters

It wasn't all better in the past, but regardless of their level, leaders are confronted with a large number of additional challenges today. Megatrends like globalization, demographic change, new ways of working, the impact of the internet, digital and social media as well as the drastically increased pace of change have a direct impact on what good leadership means today.

In an insecure environment, trust gains importance

The ancient Greek philosopher Heraclitus is supposed to have said that "the only thing that is constant is change", but at the latest in the VUCA world (volatile, uncertain, complex, ambiguous) ongoing change has become a reality in organizations. Instead of implementing a business renewal program and going back to business as usual, agility and constant transformation have become the new normal. The consequence? Environments lose stability. Requirements, job content and contacts change often. That can lead to insecurity. As a result, one leadership competency keeps groing in importance: fairness, which the Cambridge dictionary defines as "the quality of treating people equally or in a way that is right or reasonable".

Being known to be fair enables managers to successfully lead their teams through transformation.[2] It is easy to understand that employees are more willing to give their best in times of insecurity if they trust their managers. If they can be sure they will treat them fairly – rather than leave them out in the rain at the next opportunity. That requires reliability – and rules that are comprehensible and apply to everyone.

These rules must also translate into new forms of collaboration. After all, few departments still sit together from 9 to 5 in the same place. Whether this is due to international distribution, because of individual request or real estate policies with ambitious cost cutting targets, in many teams, members often work apart. This not only requires a different kind of exchange and additional alignment, it also offers a lot of opportunity for friction and misunderstanding.

Things get no easier if people come from different cultures. In that case, different views and norms impact communications, how information is interpreted and how decisions are made. With people working in one place, there was a chance that facial expressions and body language could give hints of potential misunderstandings. But physical distance can put people completely in the dark and requires new ways of orientation.

Different expectations and experience

The growing diversity of the local labor market can also challenge managers and create barriers to fair treatment. Today, teams are diverse. Members have completely different perspectives, experiences, as well as expectations and ways of life. People are of different genders, generations, nationalities and backgrounds, have different expectations for their job, their team, their employer and manager.

While diversity offers many benefits, it also regularly challenges everyone involved, because our personal demographic background also impacts our view of the world (see figure 1), our experiences and judgements. It impacts how we treat others, how we are treated and how we would like to be treated.

Leading fairly means adapting the environment and one's behaviors to meet the needs of others. That is the only way to create equal opportunities and to remove barriers that can block careers. Most of these hurdles are invisible – at least to those not confronted with them.

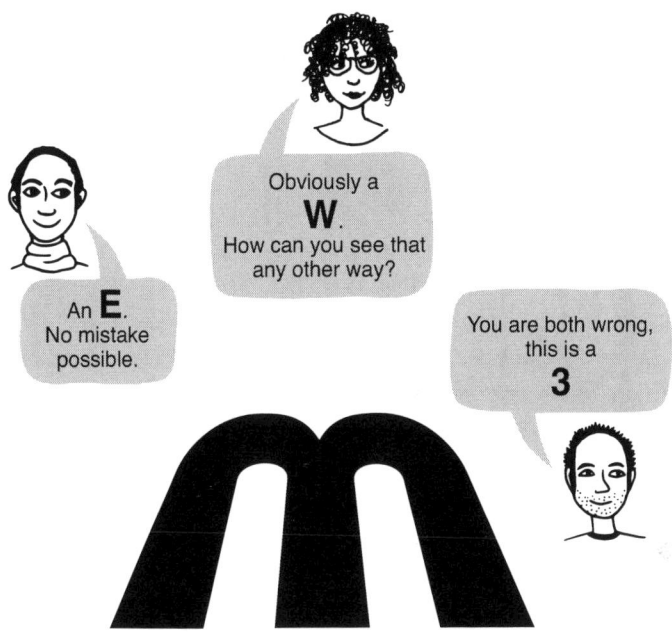

Figure 1: From different perspectives, things really do look different.

Things are rarely fair

Some examples of invisible barriers? A popular example is symphony orchestras. Until the 1970s, the share of women in the top orchestras was below 5 percent. They were considered less talented and simply unsuitable. Everyone going to a classical concert today sees a very different picture. But it was not women who have changed. Instead it took new selection procedures to ensure equal opportunities. At the so-called "blind auditions" musicians played behind screens to hide their gender – and sometimes they even came on stage in socks to avoid any telltale noises from their shoes. That measure made sure that biases did not impact judgement. Instead people were truly selected based on talent and skills. The impact was huge. Within less than 30 years, the share of women in the top five orchestras has quintupled.[3]

In spite of that success, discrimination in personnel selection remains common. Again and again, experiments in which the same CVs are sent under different names show that – in the German example – Tim Schultheiß or Lukas Heumann – stereotypically "German" sounding names – are invited way more often to interviews than Hakan Yilmaz or Ahmet Aydin – names that indicate a Turkish heritage.[4] If someone additionally wears a headscarf, they are faced with worse odds, yet. Even with a modern look, a supposed Meryem Öztürk needs to send almost five times as many applications as a Sandra Bauer to get a callback.[5] This kind of experiment has been conducted in many countries around the world, always with similar outcomes.

Sexual orientation is another factor that can create barriers. Despite the right to marry becoming the law in more and more countries, over 30 percent of gay and lesbian employees still say that they are not fully "out" at work. Especially with their managers, staff tends to be careful. Among transgender employees, as many as 70 percent hide their sexual identity at work.[6] The main reason is fear of social exclusion.[7]

This negatively impacts company results, because supposedly "private" aspects obviously influence productivity and fluctuation. If you always feel uncomfortable or see the need to make up a story when being asked about weekend activities or your family, you are unlikely to blossom at work and live up to your potential.

Thwarted

→ *Stereotypes,* prejudices and → *unconscious bias* not only impact our view of people's abilities, they also define what behaviors are considered desirable or even acceptable. At Columbia University, two CVs were distributed to students as part of a course exercise. One group was asked to evaluate a candidate called Howard, the others one called Heidi. What they did not know: both groups received the exact same CV of Heidi Roizen, a successful Silicon Valley entrepreneur and venture capitalist. Based on the students' judgment you would not have realized this. While Howard got a lot of positive evaluations, was considered a win for any organization, and seen as engaged, successful and likable, the view of Heidi was considerably less favorable. She was seen as power hungry, not sufficiently modest and too focused on her own advancement. She was judged as too aggressive for the observers' liking. I repeat: it was exactly the same CV. The only thing that influenced perception was the – unconscious – expectation of appropriate behavior for men and women.[8]

Such expectations not only impact women. They also have an impact on men, for example, if they don't meet the idea of a "typical alpha male" or if they don't put their job above everything else. Research at Yale University has shown that male CEOs who talk a lot are considered more competent than their quieter peers.[9] Men who were modest and friendly in job interviews were also judged to have violated traditional →*gender stereotypes*. The consequence? They were perceived more critically and judged less positively than women, of whom such behavior is simply expected.[10]

According to research conducted by A. T. Kearney, every second man at times experiences family requirements conflicting with their work. One in four is afraid of negative implications for his career.[11] At the same time, an Australian survey shows that men are twice as likely as women to be refused flex work, even if it is for shorter periods of time.[12]

What these examples demonstrate: instead of feeling valued and having tail wind for their career, people that differ from actual or supposed "standards" often find themselves with the wind blowing in their face. Obviously, not all differences can be seen. Many aspects that form our personality are invisible (see figure 2).

Tail wind for the career

What can companies and managers do to make sure that people shine in their jobs and can celebrate successes?

As early as the middle of the last century, Abraham Maslow, one of the fathers of humanistic psychology, pondered what people need for a fulfilled life. The Maslow hierarchy is based on five levels that describe the different needs that must be fulfilled as people strive towards self-actualization.

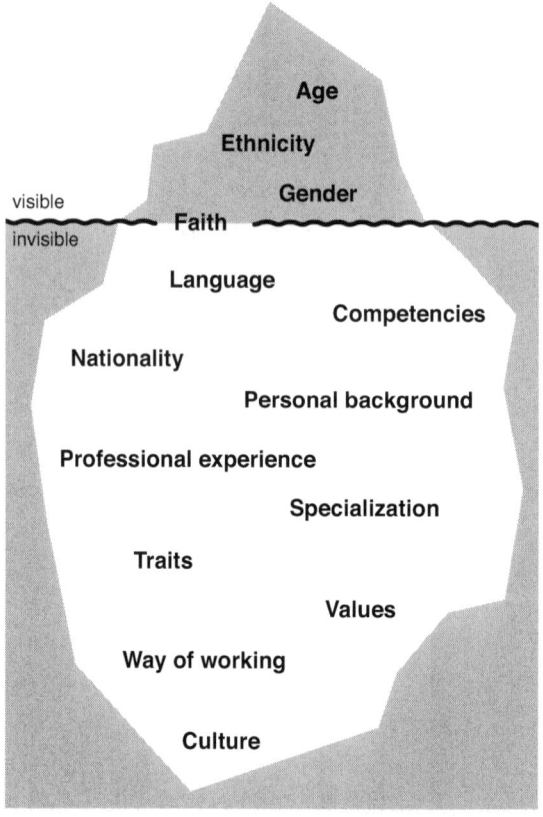

Figure 2: Many aspects that differentiate people are invisible.

Today a dynamic visualization (see figure 3) tends to be used rather than the former pyramid. After all, there is no "one after the other" or "all or nothing" relationship in our different needs. They don't have to be fulfilled 100 percent before something else gains in importance. That makes sense, also looking at our jobs. Even if one dislikes working in an open space and the computer is way too slow, it is better to be working with nice people and celebrate successes with others.

Independent of their visualization, the needs depicted by Maslow have not lost relevance. That's why it is worthwhile to take a look at the aspects that – according to Maslow – are required to be satisfied and happy. He describes five categories of needs, from elementary to

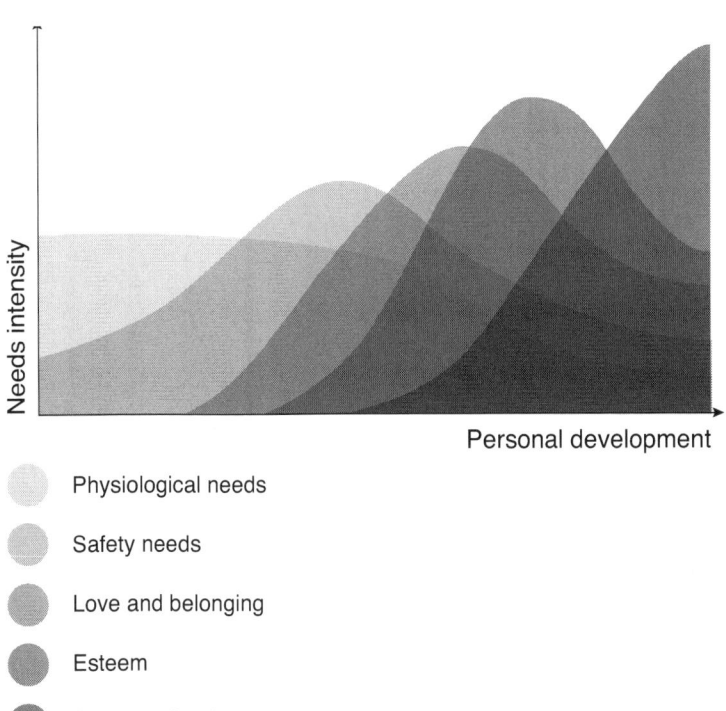

Figure 3: A dynamic visualization of the Maslow pyramid of needs

truly satisfying. Translated to the world of work, this looks something like this:

- **Physiological needs:** a pleasant workplace that fulfills basic requirements. A canteen that also offers fruits and vegetarian meals or alternatively burgers – depending on tastes.
- **Safety needs:** a job without fear, neither for your body or life. Without the experience of mobbing or bullying or being afraid of losing one's job.
- **Social needs:** a good relationship with the colleagues. Knowing that one belongs.
- **Individual needs:** Having success, standing and recognition. Feeling valued, no matter what one wants to stand for.

- **Self-actualization:** Making full use of one's potential and accomplish one's goals. Feeling stretched. Learn and grow by doing so.

Creating a fair environment

Generally, it very much depends on demographics whether or not an environment fits for someone. It depends on who one is, were they come from, the experiences they have made throughout the course of their life. Because initially, standards are set by and for the majority.

That becomes very obvious looking at the weekend: Unlike in traditionally Christian countries, Muslim majority ones tend to have their weekends on Friday and Saturday. This means that regardless of your personal faith and whether you do or don't practice it, in the vast majority of instances, the place you live will define your days off.

But those standards are not set in stone. If they no longer fit, they can be changed, even if we are talking about the weekend. What it needs? A sense that there is a problem and the will to change. Until 2013, people in Saudi-Arabia took Thursday and Friday off, which became a serious barrier for international business. How that was addressed? By royal decree the weekend was moved by one day and now follows the practices of other traditionally Muslim countries.

This book offers a new view of unfair standards and how to change them and of barriers and challenges that – literally – "others" are faced with. You will get an idea of the price that they – as well as you and your company – have to pay, and why it is worth making sure that everyone has equal opportunities. Also, you will gain insights, tools and tips on why and how to change your own behaviour and what you personally can do to create a fair and equitable environment.

To prepare for the next chapter and get even more out of it, you might want to invest a few minutes to reflect on the following questions:

- Did you ever feel that you didn't really belong? In a group, at an event or a discussion? What kind of situation was that?

- How did it feel? What went on inside you? Did you get angry or sad? Did you feel lonely or annoyed?
- What did you do? How did you deal with that situation? Did you distance yourself by putting up a wall or moving away? Did you engage even more strongly to make sure you were being heard and your view was taken into account? Did you fall silent and simply listen? Or did you just tune out?

PART 1
DAY BY DAY

The first part of the book is less about fair leadership than simply about being fair – as a manager or in day-to-day cooperation. It is about how we support others through our behavior or make life unnecessarily difficult for them.

Chapter 1, *"Get over it!"*, illustrates the power of apparently trivial behaviors that can hurt others – even unintendedly. It explores how minor actions sometimes develop a life of their own and helps to reflect one's own behaviour.

Chapter 2, *"Covering"*, is about inequities people experience because of who they are, due to personal demographics. Because they are gay or maybe black and can be put in a box because of that – even by people who consider themselves liberal and open-minded. The chapter looks at strategies that those concerned use to deal with the situation and offers advice on how to provide support.

Chapter 3, *"Birds of a feather flock together"*, takes a closer look at the concept of groups. Who we define as "us" versus "others" and how that impacts our behavior and judgement. It not only shows that our circle tends to be rather homogeneous, but also why that makes us miss out and what to do about it.

Chapter 1

Get over it!

How micro-inequities and micro-aggression stop us from having fun at work

"Next point on our agenda: our team offsite. Yasmin talked to me earlier in the corridor and she has a great idea. Come on, tell us about it", Peter nods at the young woman. She doesn't think twice and starts with verve. Peter looks at his team and beams with pride: "So? What do you think?"

It's John who speaks first. "I believe we should be looking for a setting that is more supportive of the content and agenda", he says while his boss turns towards his smartphone. "What I have been thinking…"

His eyes fixed on his phone, Peter slowly rises from his chair. "Excuse me please. I have to make a short call. Just continue without me" he says, and leaves the room.

*

"I am so sick of it!", John sits at his desk and hangs his head in resignation. "I can do whatever I want, but Peter simply ignores me. It is unfair!"

"Come on. One call. That can happen. It doesn't mean anything."

"It is not just today. You remember that big presentation last month? He asked me to send my contribution by mail but had a one-on-one meeting with Yasmin to discuss her input. Also, she was invited to attended the alignment meetings with the other departments. And I? He said he would reach out in case there were any questions."

"Maybe everything was clear?"

"Apparently not. In the end, there was virtually nothing left of my recommendations."

"Did you ask him about it?"

"Sure. I asked for a meeting. He postponed it twice and finally cancelled the third appointment completely."

Of course it exists, that painfully obvious discrimination that almost jumps into people's faces and creates an outcry of indignation. But most inequities happen differently. They occur as an endless series of tiny indications of lack of esteem.

Micro-Inequities

→ *Micro-Aggressions* or → *Micro-Inequities* are usually aimed at people who don't have a strong position in a group. Others may feel less connected with them or be upset because they are different or due to their working style. Although every individual incident might appear trivial, and can be brushed off or ignored, micro-aggressions can create deep injuries over time.

Initially, I might just be a little bit irritated because I get the impression that my ideas matter less. My manager could be writing e-mails while I am presenting in a meeting or she might be busy with something that apparently has nothing whatsoever to do with what I am saying. If I don't have an immediate response to a question, I get a shake of the head and a "you could have seen that coming and should have prepared for it". Maybe I am not invited to a working group or an event, although I'd have a lot to contribute due to my role.

Micro-aggressions can take on a multitude of different forms. When I speak up, colleagues regularly ignore my contributions. If I insist, someone rolls their eyes. There could be jokes at my cost. Nothing too serious, but it does irritate me.

Even if it's not part of my job, an unfair proportion of administrative tasks might end up at my desk. Preparing coffee, booking a conference room, quickly making some photocopies. I am sometimes forgotten on meeting invites or the rest of the team leaves for lunch without even realizing that I am missing.

For some time, I probably don't even realize what's going on. All individual incidents can be considered trivial or meaningless, could be a coincidence or a mistake, and maybe I am just being too sensitive. But while my brain is still looking for explanations, the rejection unfolds its impact subconsciously and undermines my self-confidence.

The very nature of the incidents – the fact that they appear so trivial – makes them especially destructive. If you can hardly grasp what is going on yourself, others will be blind to what is happening as well. If you experience open discrimination, you can at least hope for understanding and support. There are usually channels and rules to address the issue. If you suffer from micro-aggressions, that is unlikely.

Even family and acquaintances might react skeptically at first. "Are you sure?", "Maybe you are imagining that?", "Everyone has experienced that sort of thing" are common reactions that can stop people from taking action and addressing the issue. Instead, they remain in a situation that is increasingly becoming unbearable.

At some stage, matters develop a life of their own. Those affected tend to withdraw, become increasingly invisible and remain far below their potential. Alternatively, their reaction is to show annoyance or respond gruffly to the unfair treatment, and surprise others who have no idea where their reaction is coming from. In such cases people might be considered unstable or "angry", sulky or simply humorless. Also, they obviously don't play well in the team, because they complain about tasks which they could do to support the group. Eventually, victims of micro-aggressions will probably leave the organization or they get written off as incurably negative.

Theme	Micro-Aggression	Message
Alien in own land	"Where are you from?" "Where were you born?" "You speak good (local language)." "How do you say that in your own language?"	You are not from here. You are a foreigner.
Ascription of intelligence	"You are a credit to your race." "You are so articulate."	People of colour are generally not as intelligent as whites. It is unusual for someone of your ethnicity to be intelligent.
Criminality/assumption of criminal status	People clutching their purse or checking their wallet as someone passes. A store owner following a customer around the store A person waits to ride the next elevator.	You are a criminal. You are going to steal/ You are poor/ You do not belong. You are dangerous.
Denial of individual racism	"I'm not racist. I have several 'skin color, ethnicity' friends." "As a woman, I know what you go through as a member of a minority."	I am immune to racism because of my friends. Your oppression is no different than the one I experience. I can't be a racist. I'm like you.
Myth of meritocracy	"I believe the most qualified person should get the job." "Everyone can succeed in this society, if they work hard enough."	If organizations take personal demographics into account, it creates an unfair advantage for members of minority groups. People that don't make it here are lazy, they need to try harder or are simply not smart enough.
Pathologizing cultural values/ communication styles	Asking a black person: "Why do you have to be so loud/animated? Just calm down." To someone of south-east Asian descent: "Why are you so quiet? We want to know what you think. Be more verbal." "Speak up more."	Assimilate to dominant culture.

Table 1: Examples of xenophobia and racial micro-aggressions[13]

You can be accidentally unfair

It is important to realize that micro-inequities can impact those concerned way beyond the apparently "trivial" nature of individual incidents. Often the initiator does not even realize what he or she is doing. After all, they might not even be acting intentionally. It is not necessarily about putting an especially annoying colleague in his place or using a well-timed joke to strengthen one's own position.

Micro-inequities can happen unintendedly and can be directed against people we don't even know. That's what happens if stereotypes or our unconscious preferences and biases take over. People with foreign roots often make that experience when they are asked in their home countries where they are from "for real". While it might be well intended as a sign of interest in another person, it often comes across as "you don't really belong" (see table 1).

Describing a scene from the German TV show "The Super Talent" journalist Ferda Ataman calls it an "ethnic sorting fad".[14] The host, not satisfied with the response of a small girl telling him she is from Herne, a town in the west of Germany, keeps asking about her parents and even grandparents. "The interesting thing about the scene: The little girl does not even know what that man is talking about. Two worlds are clashing, and it can't be explained by 60 years difference in age only. Apparently, little Melissa, that is the name of the girl, did not start her career as an 'Asian German'. She had truly believed she was from Herne and from Germany. Sadly enough, she will have ample opportunities during the course of her life to understand that this is not the case."[15]

Another example: In Western society with its preference for extroversion, introverted people are also regularly made to feel that they don't fully comply. Well-meaning advice like "you should be more outgoing" or "don't be so distant" in essence sends the message that their personal style is not compatible with what is desirable and they had better be different.[16]

It is also an attack on the self-image of the IT-savvy senior citizen if she is told "you are doing this well and despite your age!". Although she easily masters the challenges of modern technology, she is made fully aware that there were good reasons to have doubts about that. The apparent compliment is poisoned. Through no fault of her own, she is confronted with an uphill battle and has to demonstrate competence and capabilities towards a skeptical audience. Most likely, many of us know that this is considerably more difficult than starting out from a position of strength and trust in your abilities.

Gender inclusive language

There is increasing discussion of the role of the language we use in creating an equitable environment. This is broader than the questions of the right pronoun to use to address those of us that don't identify as man or woman. Nonetheless, gender non-binary is something everyone should make themselves more familiar with. After all, 35 percent of members of Generation Z – those born since 1997 – know someone who prefers to be addressed by a gender-neutral pronoun.[17] Also, lawmakers are increasingly acknowledging that it is discriminating and hurting people in their fundamental rights if, for example, they can't register with a positive gender attribute beyond man or woman.[18]

The increasing diversity of genders is a topic many people struggle with, and consider difficult to understand. While this book is not the space to dive into the topic in any depth, at least I want to provide a model (figure 4) that I personally find extremely helpful. It helps familiarize oneself with the topic and what it comprises. That it is not all about biology. It is also related to the gender we identify with and how strongly we do. About the gender of those that we are attracted to sexually or that we fall in love with. And finally about the way that we present ourselves. The way we dress, what we project to the outside world and how that expression is interpreted by others due to the gender norms of the society we live in.[19]

But even just looking at women and men, a lot remains to be done. Because most languages are neither as neutral nor as specific as many tend to believe. While English appears to be gender-neutral, research increasingly demonstrates that this is far from true.

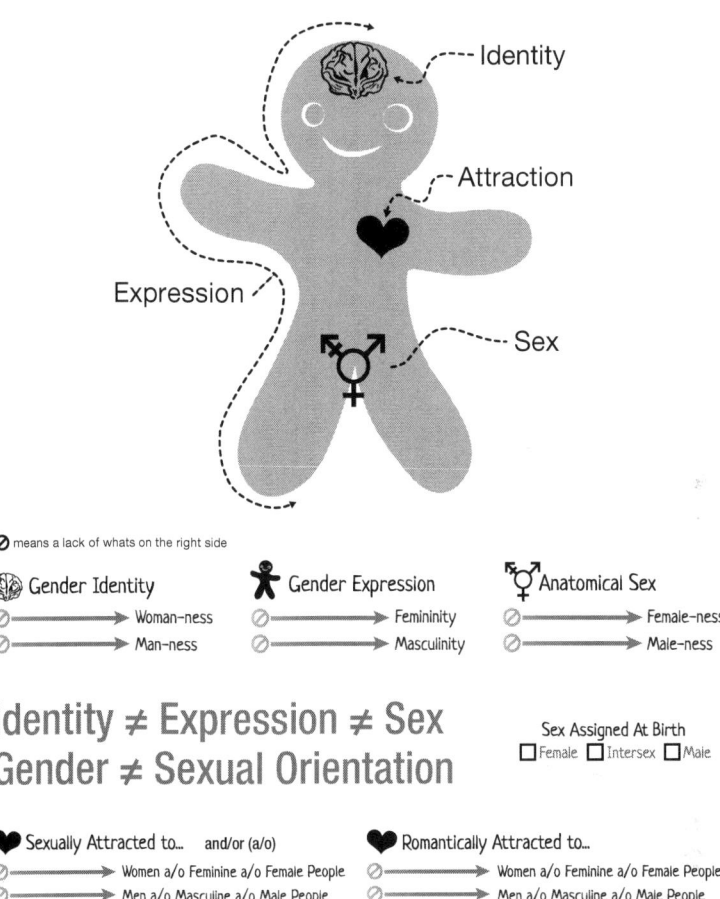

Figure 4: The Genderbread Person, by Sam Killerman, www.genderbread.org

Stereotypes directly impact our perception and expectations despite an allegedly gender neutral language. Experiments show that people automatically think of a man if someone refers to a "doctor", "lawyer" or "expert". If it is actually a woman one is referring to, that fact is often highlighted by mentioning they are "female experts" or "female astronauts", thereby reinforcing the notion that the standard person in a high-powered and high-status job is a man. That's why creating gender equity requires generally stating the gender of the person – even if that is perceived as complicated or a long-winded way of speaking.

The German language, on the other hand, offers terms that reflect the gender of the person one is talking about. A teacher – "ein Lehrer" – has a female counterpart – "eine Lehrerin". And then there is the so called "generic masculine" – meaning that the male version can be used to refer to either men or women. Grammatically, it is supposed to be a neutral way of speaking without any gender ascription. But that is not true. While there are just as strong stereotypes in regards to "men's" and "women's" occupations in Germany, grammar overwrites them completely.[20] If someone uses the generically masculine and supposedly gender-neutral term "Vorschullehrer" (preschool teacher), respondents overwhelmingly think of a man, although it is a stereotypically female role. It is at best only after some reflection that they recognize it could also be a woman who is being referred to.

That's why it is extremely important to use gender-inclusive speech, regardless of the language one actually uses. Failing to do so is a micro-aggression. It is as if you were coming to a party where everyone gets a handshake and you don't even earn a simple nod. It is as if you were invisible. That is not just impolite. It sustains gender stereotypes and imbalance, because even children are aware of the ambiguity.

Men's jobs? Women's jobs?

Researchers in Berlin wanted to understand whether language could be used to reduce gender stereotypes in the jobs people chose. Whether using a language that shines a light on the fact that jobs perceived as "typically male" could also be performed by women would impact perceptions of kids.

To do so, they read job titles to children between 6 and 12, either using the male and female form or alternatively the "generic masculine" plural. The outcome was absolutely clear. Children who heard about the role of a "female or male engineer" ("Ingenieurinnen / Ingenieure") or "female or male auto mechanic" ("Automechanikerinnen

/Automechaniker") were way more likely to believe they were up to a job in which women are currently underrepresented.[21] If just the male plural form was used, professions were perceived as more difficult and harder to learn. Those jobs were seen – according to their own judgement – as less suitable for girls. After all, girls lose faith in their ability to master big challenges early on.

In one experiment, children between five and seven were read a story with a "very, very smart" main character without any indication of his or her gender. Afterwards, they were asked to identify that protagonist out of four photographs – two with women, two with men. At the age of five, both, girls and boys selected a person of their own gender. At six and seven, boys as well as girls were more likely to select a photograph of a man. At the same age, girls were beginning to lose interest in games that were said to require them to be especially smart. Instead they began to focus on the ones that needed a lot of effort.[22] This demostrates that being clearly addressed is an important confidence booster for girls.

Also it shows that it is not sufficient to act only when one personally recognizes the need to do so. Whether my behaviour is OK or not is less about me and what I think than how it impacts others. Often, I am not even aware of the consequences of what I do or say. That makes it even more important to be very open to feedback and take criticism into account even if I don't consider it very relevant myself.

Tipps for dealing with micro-aggressions

Scrutinize your own behaviour. Consider whether you might be hurting others unintentionally. Maybe there are even people you systematically keep small.

Get active. Observe what goes on e.g. in meetings and create a level playing field. Invite people to speak who don't get that space although they clearly want to contribute. Show interest and appreciation.

Reach out to people that are hurting others – even if unintentionally – and make them aware of their behavior and that you won't accept it.

Avoid questions or compliments that are based on stereotypes. If something surprises you, consider what that might say about you and your world view, versus expressing your thoughts without reflection.

Chapter 2
Covering

What it means when you can't be who you are at work

"Do you know that one? A gay man enters a bar..." Linda giggles in anticipation of the fabulous punch line and her colleagues can hardly wait. Only John is not amused.

"What is it? Do you have a problem?"

"That is not funny. It is homophobic."

"Seriously? Spoilsport! A friend of mine is gay and he thinks it is funny, too. Also, he says that the whole political correctness thing is way overboard. It must be OK to have some fun!"

In theory, it is possible to joke about anything, but that's not what happens in the real world. Anyone reflecting on their personal repertoire will quickly come to realize that themselves. While jokes provide a great opportunity to bridge differences and celebrate communalities, they are often used as weapons. Aristoteles was already aware that humor was a way to demonstrate supremacy.[23]

There are jokes about blondes and hairdressers who obviously cannot count up to three. Medical personnel and fire fighters on the other hand – occupations enjoying high esteem – find themselves as a target of insiders at best. Also, jokes about bankers only gained popularity when their image took a blow during the banking crisis. Jokes to heighten your status celebrate stereotypes, negative ones. Of course you may find that funny. But do you have to?

Humor has many facets

The psychologist Rod A. Martin identifies four styles of humor that have very different implications (Table 2). Humor can be used to strengthen relationships (*affiliative*), pick oneself up (*self-enhancing*), it can be at the cost of others (*aggressive*) or aimed against oneself (*self-defeating*).

Affiliative	Using humor to foster group cohesion: telling jokes and making fun of things that everybody can safely laugh at and feel included in good fellowship. Non-hostile, non-competitive and benign humor style. This kind of humor also helps to resolve tension in a group and avoid conflict.
Self-enhancing	A tendency to be amused by various things in one's life, also when faced with difficult or stressful situations. It can be viewed as a skill used to cope with stress in a proactive way.
Aggressive	Using humor to disparage, manipulate or threaten others; it is destructive for group cohesion and can lead to in-group divisions and cause certain individuals to suffer.
Self-defeating	Involves allowing others to make jokes at one's cost and pretending that one's having fun along the way. There is also a tendency to use self-deprecating humor to amuse others e.g. in anticipation of them hurting you, to hide your true feelings or in an attempt to be accepted as part of a group.

Table 2: Four different humor styles according to Rod A. Martin [24]

Why does that matter? Because →*psychological safety* is a key factor for the performance of a team. We judge situations intuitively, at a subconscious level. If we feel insecure or threatened, it activates a "fight or flight" reaction. We prepare for battle or a very fast retreat. Neither is a great precondition for creativity and productive collaboration.

We are only able to concentrate on the task at hand and contribute to our best ability when our mind tells us "it is OK, nobody is going to hurt you". That's why making jokes at the expense of others disturbs group cohesion and undermines success.[25] And on top of that: it is simply not kind.

It might be disappointing to miss out on that fabulous punch line, that brilliant response that would demonstrate just how quick-witted you are and gets people on your side. But many jokes are examples of micro-aggressions, too. That's why it is worthwhile to consider whether your personal gain justifies the prize that others have to pay – because you hurt them, because group cohesion suffers or stereotypes are reinforced.

Words hurt

Jokes are often defended by complaining about excessive "political correctness", that it still must be "OK to say things like that" or by telling others they have no sense of humor. Whoever feels hurt if they are laughed about, or even complains, can't expect a lot of compassion. "It's just a joke" or "don't make such a big deal out of it" are common reactions.

Anyone who thinks that way is in good company. "You shouldn't say whatever comes to mind", says Wolfgang Huber, a former Protestant German Bishop, in an interview. Yet he complains about the "strong tendency towards political correctness, including strict rules for gender-neutral language. This leads to a narrowing of the public debate".[26][27] What he overlooks is that people who feel limited by political correctness are usually the ones who aren't normally the victims of condescending or hurtful remarks. Accordingly, they lack the experience of what it feels like and what it does to people.

A study by the US Pew Research Centers[28] demonstrates that point clearly. They explored how acceptable people from different nationalities considered offensive speech. The highest level of acceptance was found in the US, where 77 percent of respondents support the right of others to make statements that are offensive to their own religious beliefs. More than two thirds think people should be allowed to make public statements that are offensive to minority groups, again the highest percentage in the poll. Those concerned have quite a different perspective, though. While 38 percent of respondents from other ethnicities than white think the government should be able to prevent people from making statements that are offensive to minority groups, just 23 percent of whites hold that view. Instead, they tend to believe that "too many people are easily offended these days over the language that others use." In 2016, 59 percent of Americans agreed with that statement – and even 83 percent of those who voted for Donald Trump.

Looking at different generations, there is hope, though. It shows that societal change and exposure to "others" creates empathy and changes perception. While just 12 percent of the so called "Silent Generation" (those born between 1925 and 1945) think the government should be able to prevent offensive statements, 40 percent of Millennials (born between 1981 and 1996) hold that view.

Another popular argument, knowing someone "diverse" who shares our perspective – whether a gay friend, a women hating her female manager, a Muslim criticizing Islam – also does not hold weight. Instead it is a sign of a lack of familiarity with (groups of) people. In that case the view of one individual is sufficient to support our stereotypical view.

Anyone who knows several people belonging to a certain "group" is more likely to avoid generalization, because this increases the awareness of their diversity and the broad range of experiences and perspectives they have.

Covering

There is another aspect that can disguise what is truly going on: the so-called "→ *covering*". This means that people hide part of their personality because they have no interest to engage in the same discussions over and over again and want to avoid a single factor about them gaining massive importance when it should be irrelevant. A prominent example of this was US president Franklin D. Roosevelt. He always made sure that he was already seated at the table when his cabinet entered the room. He needed a wheelchair to get about and everyone knew that. Still, he didn't want to remind them of that fact, instead making sure it did not influence the discussion.

I personally had one of my most extreme covering moments at a sales meeting. I got along fabulously with my colleagues – all men – and it was important for me to be accepted as "one of them". After the formal part of the meeting had ended, they decided to have some fun and move about town. Being invited to come along felt like an accolade. That evening ended at a strip club.

Today, I'd know how to deal with that kind of incident. Go along and remain in charge of the situation, find allies or simply persuade my colleagues to go for a different kind of entertainment. At that stage, it was awful. Especially when one of them had the brilliant idea that I should get a lap dance. I was in a Catch-22 situation. I didn't want to hurt the relationship with them at any cost. I wanted to be part of the group and apparently, those were the rules. Leave and be made fun of afterwards? Absolutely impossible. Luckily, the dancer found one of the men way more interesting than me, which put an end to that awkward incident.

Going along, remaining silent and making concessions in order not to hurt relationships are common forms of covering. These behaviors are not just displayed by people who regularly experience discrimination because of personal attributes, 45 percent of white heterosexual men say that they have covered.[29] That doesn't mean they generally feel excluded. They just see the need to comply with certain rules not of their own making to be part of a group or organization. There are conditions for their belonging. Not to comply would threaten social cohesion.

There are four axes along which individuals can cover to comply with group norms:

- Appearance-based: altering one's self-presentation to blend into the mainstream.
- Affiliation-based: avoiding behaviors widely associated with one's identity, often to negate stereotypes.

- Advocacy-based: how much individuals "stick up for" their group.
- Association-based: avoiding contact with other group members.

I already mentioned that almost 70 percent of transgender employees hide their sexual identity at work. But they are by far not the only ones that hide aspects about themselves. A prominent example is Margaret Thatcher, who underwent an extensive makeover prior to her election as UK prime minister. She was a woman from the middle class, not the best precondition for the highest office. To hide her origin, she completely overhauled her attire, her hair cut and wardrobe. And because her voice was considered shrill, she worked with a speech coach at the Royal National Theatre, to lower her pitch and develop a more authoritative tone.

A German example is Philip Amthor, a member of Angela Merkel's Christian Democrat Party. He is known for his conservative positions, traditional clothing and jokes that one might expect from a man several times his age. He is one of the youngest members of parliament but behaves as if he were one of the oldest. Seeing his very obvious career ambitions, it is probably a smart move. Two out of three employees in Germany prefer their managers to be older than themselves – a higher score than their European neighbors – and public servants belong to the more traditionalist audiences.[30]

While "too young" can be a barrier, "old" is actually the most common ground for discrimination in Europe.[31] Older employees are judged as less healthy, less motivated and rather resistant to change. They are considered neither interested nor truly able to succeed in a fast-paced work environment. While there is no empirical evidence for most of the prejudices against older employees[32], they still experience less appreciation, declining trust in their abilities and have lower chances of being hired or promoted.[33]

Not a good idea, as 20-first CEO Avivah Wittenberg-Cox highlights: "Half the children born today have a 50 percent chance of living to 105. That's up from 1 percent a century ago. While the debate about exactly how long we can hope to live rages on, it's likely to be a lot longer than any of us are prepared for. And as our lifespan extends, so our "healthspan" is likely also to improve, leaving us healthier, both physically and mentally, for much longer. This has implications for every dimension of life – but one of the things it will impact most is our current conception, definition, and expectations of what a career looks like."[34]

In the current climate, though, older employees often react in a similar way: In anticipation of common prejudices, they make jokes about age, trying to distance themselves from their peer group. Generally, that strategy does not pay off, instead reinforcing negative stereotypes about age.[35]

Alternatively, people take care not to behave in a way that gets them put in a box. This can mean that elderly people or those with a handicap try to fully engage in sports activities despite limitations they might have, because they are afraid of being hurt by negative group stereotypes – biases or concerns about "people like them" – and of being perceived as less capable in general. Mothers don't mention at work that they need go and pick up their children, in order to avoid comments like "taking half the day off again?" and the impression that they might be less committed to the job than their childless peers.

It can also be covering if you avoid advocating for a topic you care about. In such cases you might laugh at sexist, homophobic or racist jokes, to avoid having to confront others who apparently have no issue at all with that behaviour. Often, those concerned also don't speak up for people who look like them. If you are not part of the mainstream, you might be expected to support others "like you", but if you do, your motives are regularly questioned. It is often believed that a recommendation is based on a shared background rather than the qualification of the candidate. This reduces the value of your recommendation and can even hurt your own reputation.

Covering can also mean avoiding contact with people, with whom you have obvious things in common. That strategy is often used, if someone wants to ensure that negative group stereotypes don't reflect back on them after they have finally managed to distance themselves from those perceptions and are perceived as individuals with their own qualities and behaviors. Also, they might want to avoid the perception of forming huge uniform masses bent on societal upheaval and a revolution. Sometimes the fear seems to be overwhelming. The first time I sat on a management team together with another woman, our boss regularly sat us apart. Apparently, he was completely overwhelmed by that massive female presence concentrated on one spot at the table. The many, many men didn't even register with him.

Covering is expensive for everyone

Should your response to all this be "So what? All of us have to comply with certain rules", you are underestimating the issue. People who believe that it is not themselves who is being accepted and valued, but only an adapted, streamlined version, are not only in secret conflict with their environment. They are also locked in an inner conflict because hiding part of one's identity hurts the image that people have of themselves.

Hints of what is expected are given by managers. They play an overwhelming role in creating a culture in which everyone is being valued. With their behavior they demonstrate what rules exist for a team. What is expected and OK and what behaviors are unacceptable. Everyone who feels required to adapt their behavior and to cover part of who they are based on these signs will also see fewer opportunities for themselves in that team. After all, it is apparently neither intended nor desired that people like them are successful. That impacts personal engagement, performance and the results of a team.

Tips for exploring new perspectives

<u>Become aware of the rules of your team.</u> Looking at your team, what commonalities are apparent? Both in terms of demographics as well as interests. How does that impact rules and dealings with each other? Who could be disadvantaged because of that? What can you do to include them more fully?

<u>Plan for activities that everybody enjoys.</u> Make sure that everyone enjoys common undertakings. If you can't reach consensus, don't

just follow the majority vote. Consider whether concerns beyond "this is boring" might keep people from taking part. Take special care if it is always the same people that are outvoted.

Avoid and actively address statements that could hurt others. No joke is worth the price of hurting others. That quick laugh you earn can leave serious wounds.

Sharpen your perception. Reach out to "other" people and approach them actively. This can help you explore new perspectives and to get a very different understanding of their experiences and opinions.

Chapter 3

Birds of a feather flock together

Why our existing network is rarely future-proof and how to develop it systematically

Yasmin looks at her Twitter feed entirely stunned:

"Did you chose your husband yourself?" I am sick of that question. Just like "Where do you come from?"

*

I don't understand what you are complaining about. Asking where one is coming from is a common question. Everyone gets asked that. It is a sign of interest and a good opening.

*

As far as I know, it is still difficult for woman to marry someone who isn't from Turkey. The parents usually try stop that. I even saw a documentary on TV. That's why I don't see any issue with that question.

*

Everybody truly devoted to Islam should also accept shari'ah, stoning, circumcision, forced marriage and separate entrances to the mosque. Everything else is anti-Islam. No backtalk!

*

Obviously you dislike the question "where do you come from?" if you are ashamed of your ancestors.

*

Seriously? What is your idea of small talk and getting to know someone? Limiting yourself to the weather???

*

Well, what do you say? Did you choose your husband yourself? Doesn't even matter. You don't belong here and never will. Period.

*

I can clearly see who is from here and who doesn't belong. It is not as if I had just taken a holiday here. We have lived here for generations and that's why I can tell.

*

It is like having guests at home. If they misbehave, you don't just accept that. You intervene – unless you are dumb. A loser and complete failure. But if you do, you are called racist. Sick.

*

Integration means that guests adapt to the local customs without complaining or making requests. That's doubly true for anyone who is born here.

I have already addressed the idea of "people like us" and "others" in the previous chapters. Also, how painful it can be if someone feels excluded. In this chapter, I want to take a closer look at the concept of "groups". Who we know and who we like. Why most people have a relatively homogeneous circle of acquaintances, why it is worth changing that and how to do it.

In- and Out-Group

During the course of our lives, all of us are part of different groups. Often, this has nothing to do with actual memberships that we actively engage in. At least as important are sociodemographic factors – like age, gender, family status, where we live, ethnicity and so on – as well as socioeconomic aspects like educational background and income.

All of these aspects impact the experiences we are likely to have, the decisions we take and they impact our values and our view of the world. It makes a difference whether we are born in Brussels or Beijing, in 1960 or 1990. Whether our parents believed we'd go to university or would have to rely on social welfare. It is our environment that teaches us what is OK, how to get by, what is desirable and what is embarrassing. It also impacts who we are surrounded by – at school, in associations, clubs and cliques.

The people with whom we share important aspects, experiences or interests form our →*In-Group*. And we are part of more than one. I could be from a capital city, have graduated from a famous school, work at a great company, be a member of the Rotary Club and a fervent supporter of my local soccer club. All of these traits connect me to some and differentiate me from others. Because they might be from a small town, have gone to a different school, work for a competitor, not belong to a similarly exclusive circle, and are fans of Manchester United.

It is so important for us to be part of a group that trivial factors can be enough to make us feel that we belong. In one experiment, participants felt connected based on how good people were at guessing the number of sweets in a glass. Those guessing too high were certain that they had more in common with other "overraters" than with the "underraters" among them.[36] Even the outcome of tossing a coin can be sufficient to make one feel part of a group.[37]

People different from us, belong to the →*Out-Group*. We have reservations about them and distance ourselves from them. Because we feel superior or inferior. Because we don't "get them", because they behave strangely or in conflict with our own preferences or belief. Sometimes it also simply helps to confirm our own decisions. Mothers with paid jobs versus those managing the family at home. Men focused on their careers versus those strongly engaged in their family. "Blokes" vs. "wimps". This phenomenon is called →*outgroup derogation*.

Privileges

Being part of the "right" group comes with →*privileges*. That does not mean a silver spoon or a private jet. Instead, it gives you advantages over others in some situations or in a specific context that have nothing to do with any personal achievements.

In Germany, children of parents with a university degree are three times more likely to attend higher education than young adults whose parents have completed vocational training.[38] With a mother or father having a degree or a leadership position in a big company, they are also more likely to have access to first-hand reports about university courses and their challenges, to role models working in professions that require a degree and a stronger conviction that they can make it too. They might even know people who can help them get an internship or a job interview.

One's background is also a defining factor in whether and where one can find a place to live. In Germany, Lena Meyer is more likely to get an appointment to view a flat than Ayse Gülbeyaz – especially in the nice parts of town.[39] Even the price of buying is impacted by one's roots. In the US, Countrywide Financial Corporation was fined $335 million, for systematically offering loans with higher charges and interest rates to African-American and Hispanic borrowers.[40]

"Black Lives Matter" has created increasing awareness in the US for the privileges of white Americans. Aspects being highlighted include questions like "do I need to tell my kid how to react if pulled over by the police for fear of them being shot?", "can I swear, wear second hand clothing, or not respond to letters without my decisions being attributed to bad morals, poverty, lack of education or the color of my skin?", "are 'skin-colored band aids' actually the color of my skin?" or "are people of my race fairly represented on TV and in newspapers?".

If I am part of a privileged group, 'people like me' are more likely to play a leading role in a movie. The Bechdel test is a measure that helps evaluate the relative status accorded to men and women. Based on three simple questions, it analyses whether men and women are at eye level or whether old fashioned stereotypes are reinforced. To pass the test, (1) a film has to have at least two women in it, who (2) talk to each other, about (3) something besides a man. In 2013, almost half the films still failed that simple test.[41]

That can't be explained by expectations of the audience or commercial considerations. While films with strong women tend to be produced on a smaller budget, they actually provide more bang for the buck. On average, movies that pass the Bechdel test have a higher gross profit per invested dollar.[42]

In real life, too, men are often the yardstick by which others are measured – often unknowingly or unintentionally. They enjoy the perfect climate at the office – and not just metaphorically. The optimal room temperature has been defined based on the metabolic rate of men. As women's is significantly lower, they are often cold and need a scarf to weather the environment.

Also, although women are less often involved in accidents, they are hurt more badly when it does happen. That is even taking into account factors like the seriousness of the accident and whether a seatbelt was used. As women are smaller than men on average, their seats tend to be pushed forward. Engineers consider this a 'nonstandard position' which results in a higher risk of inner injuries and injuries of the legs.[43]

It can also be dangerous for women that the pharmaceutical industry still tends to test drugs predominantly on men. That is despite the fact that the bodies of men and women have some glaring differences. The result: active agents dispense very differently and women are 1.5 times more likely to suffer unintended side effects that can range from headaches to circulatory shock. Still, the number of drugs that are tested on females is increasing only slowly. The fact that women are not simply smaller and lighter men makes it complicated. Due to changing levels of hormones during the female cycle and menopause, more participants have to be included for reliable results to be obtained. Also, it hurts comparisons with previous studies that were only based on men. That's why there is a tendency to hold on to outdated standards despite better knowledge.[44]

One easy way to become aware of one's privileges can be to use Twitter. Following people with lives and backgrounds different from your own can provide glimpses into their lives and how their experiences differ. How everyday occurrences and even the reaction to their tweets are not at all the same as with you. That even neutral comments can result in heavy criticism and malice. How stereotypes and prejudices impact the exchange.

This provides a fabulous opportunity for everyone who is not sure whether they would have the courage or take the time to stand in for others in a face to face situation. Twitter is an easy and low barrier test field. Drinking your first cup of coffee in the morning, you can already help provide a counterweight to a discussion and support people faced with discrimination. If enough people get involved, a single positive comment or like can already help make a difference. And it might even provide the required impetus also to act in real life.

Birds of a feather flock together

One of the reasons we are blind to our own privileges is that we take them for granted. It is our "normal". It is much like tailwind when riding a bike. If we don't see trees or branches moving, we don't even recognize that our wild ride is not simply the result of our strong pedaling and personal performance, but that we are helped along by the wind. A similar cross check with outside factors – the reality of other people – is rarely conducted with regard to our privileges.

One of the reasons is → *social homophily*, the fact that we predominantly know people who are similar to ourselves and share the same experiences. The phrase "birds of a feather flock together" describes the fact that most people around us tend to have a lot in common in terms of background, education and social status, and we predominantly seek contacts with people who "fit". This impacts our private as well as business networks, our circle of friends and acquaintances, our partnerships and who we support with practical help and good advice.[45] It means surrounding ourselves with people who are "like us", who share our views and prevent us from questioning our perspectives at times.

That is the kind of network that Herminia Ibarra, a professor at the London Business School, calls 'narcissistic and lazy'. The kind of network that forms spontaneously and naturally with no added efforts required, comprised of people who meet automatically and immediately click. But these networks are usually homogenous and offer little value. "These networks can never give us the breadth and diversity of inputs we need to understand the world around us, to make good decisions and to get people who are different from us on board with our ideas. That's why we should develop our professional networks deliberately, as part of an intentional and concerted effort to identify and cultivate relationships with relevant parties."[46]

Not knowing "others" is expensive

Among others, the Center for Talent Innovation has explored the impact of different perspectives on coming up with great ideas. It found that the probability of a team developing relevant solutions increases massively if just one member shares key demographic traits – like gender, ethnicity, generation or national culture – with the target audience.[47]

People who rely on a few close confidants reduce their own opportunities. Many experiments demonstrate that people who are close to us tend to have access to the same information and ideas we already have. That's why their advice is less valuable. As early as the 1970s, Sociologist Mark Granovetter proved what he called "the strength of weak ties". In his experiment "Getting a Job" he found that a lot of people find a new job through contacts they have. But this happend rarely – just in 17 percent of cases – through people they saw frequently. Almost three out of ten found a job through someone they hardly ever met.[48] These "weak ties" connect out network with people and groups very different from the ones we usually associate with.

This was exactly the finding of Jeffrey Travers and Stanley Milgram.[49] They wanted to explore the "small world problem" in pre-LinkedIn times and to find out whether everybody knows everyone else via just a few degrees of separation. They asked 300 test subjects in Boston and Nebraska to send a letter to a person unknown to them who was based in Massachusetts. To that aim, they should send the letter to acquaintances, asking them to forward it until it finally reached its destination. None of the letters that actually did reach the intended recipient needed more than six stops. But only 64 got there at all. The majority of letters simply circulated in the close vicinity of their departure because the initial sender didn't know anyone outside their local environment.

This situation has changed less than might be expected over the last 50 years. Even in social media, connections are largely homogeneous. Though we are more internationally connected and meeting a more diverse range of people, we do not leverage these opportunities and resources. In her executive development programs, Ibarra finds again and again that the majority of participants have their contacts within their own discipline, sector or company. External perspectives are rarely used, even when discussing strategic questions.

On the other hand she comes across people that have almost their complete network outside their immediate work environment. While that is great when looking for a new job externally, strong internal ties are needed to implement new ideas and solutions within one's own organization.

One typical blind spot are connections with people further down in the hierarchy. With all that effort to climb the corporate ladder and position oneself vis-à-vis key stakeholders, many participants overlook the importance of strong ties with those who know how "regular employees" feel and what matters to them. That's why a strong network offers a 360 degree perspective and includes contacts at a lower, higher and the same level as oneself.[50]

And now?

To identify weaknesses in one's own network, it is worth to conducting a comprehensive analysis that looks at breadth and diversity, connectivity and dynamics. The starting point is an overview of your most important contacts. To that end, create a list of those people who you have recently asked for advice or have used as a sparring partner.

Keep your network broad

In the next step, review the connectivity and concentration of your network, whether most of your key contacts are also familiar with each other or move in different circles. That way you can validate whether you have enough "connectors", people who provide access to other networks.

To find out, simply enter the names of your key contacts in an overview like table 4 and add a cross if people are also acquainted with each other. I case you don't know, leave that field empty.

	2	3	4	5	6	7	8	9	10
1.									
2.									
3.									
4.									
5.									
6.									
7.									
8.									
9.									
10.									

Table 4: Understanding network density

If you want, you can even calculate the network density and track how it changes with new contacts:

1. Count the number of contacts on the list.
2. Multiply their number (n) with n-1 and divide the result by 2.
3. Count the number of crosses in the matrix and divide their number by the result from 2. That is your network density
   A low network density indicates a broad network.[51]

Keep your network diverse

To identify which perspectives might be missing from your network, it helps to use an overview like table 5. That allows you to map important aspects of your contacts – with regard to their demography as well as their role. You can track whether they work in- or outside your organization, at what level, as well as their function and industry – whether it is your own or a different one that can help you gain important insights. Additionally, you can create transparency as to whether people of different genders, generations, nationalities, ethnicities and so on are part of your network and reasonably represented.

Such an overview provides a quick and very clear insight into the diversity of key contacts and what aspects might be missing.

	Gender	Age group	Nationality	Other aspects*	
Contact 1					
Contact 2					
Contact 3					
...					

Table 5: Matrix to analyse the diversity of your network* e.g. ethnicity, inside or outside your orgnization, function, industry, level, and so on

Keep your network fresh and dynamic

A dynamic network ensures that your contacts stay relevant and helpful. To that end, it is insufficient to simply rely on existing relationships. Because of changing tasks or roles, as we advance or change companies, and due to developments in our environment, contacts can get old and don't necessarily align with our business realities any longer. Also, the growing diversity of the work environment means that a homogeneous network which might have been just great in the past, is insufficient today. A diverse network has an added strength: Due to social homophily, actively reaching out to people unlike yourself is very likely to increase the number of weak ties and also connect you with other groups.

Future-proofing your network requires a comprehensive strategy. The starting point should be your goals: where do you want to be in a few years' time? What do you want to achieve? What do you enjoy? Don't simply rely on your own inspiration. Talk to your contacts about strengths and learning fields as well as any ideas and suggestions they might have.

As soon as you are clear about your vision and know what you are aiming for, it is a good idea to create a three-step networking action plan.[52]

- Step 1: define goals that will help you achieve your vision.
- Step 2: connect these goals with people, tools etc., that will help you realize them.
- Step 3: identify the best way to build relationships with those people.

This helps to develop your network in a targeted way. At step 2, it is worth going back to the matrix you made that indicates the breadth of your network. This way you can validate whether your current contacts will be sufficient to achieve your vision and which perspectives are probably missing. You might even get completely new ideas and inspirations.

One great way to develop new and relevant contacts is *Working Out Loud*[53]. Here, the leading principle is generosity. Rather than reaching out to people for help, the idea is to explore the actions you can take in order to support them. Contributions you can make, which can be simple as a "like" for a post, a comment or recommendation. You can share information or an article they might find useful. You can ask a question to give them a chance to respond and shine. That way an exchange is initiated. Over time, visibility and trust increase and contributions can become increasingly meaningful, leading to stronger mutual support and the ability to achieve more together.

Tips to increase the diversity of your network

<u>Analyse your network.</u> Take a critical look to understand where you usually seek advice and whether the perspectives you take into account are truly aligned with current realities.

<u>Follow people on Twitter and LinkedIn that are very different from yourself.</u> Leverage social media to gain new perspectives and insights into the realities of other people.

Get involved in the conversation. Whether on- or offline, look for opportunities to participate in discussions you might not usually be involved in. It tends to be a good idea to start by listening.

Move outside your comfort zone. Attend events that you would not normally have on your agenda.

Simply listen. In dialogs, we invest a lot of energy into thinking about what to say next, into formulating our thoughts and identifying the moment that it is "our turn". Simply listening allows you to fully concentrate on the other person and learn so much more.

PART 2
TEAM WORK

The next chapters are all about collaboration within a team and group dynamic processes that are relevant in that context.

Chapter 4, *"No one could possibly have seen that coming!"*, explores one of the biggest issues of homogeneous teams, the lack of different perspectives and groupthink. This results in important information missing or being ignored and leads to worse decision making.

Chapter 5, *"You always do that exceptionally well!"*, looks at how different tasks are often distributed in teams. While some get the chance to shine as they work on strategic projects with high visibility, others – independently of their role – tend to get stuck with tasks with little prestige.

Chapter 6, *"Could you quickly give me a hand?"*, explores advantages and limitations of collaboration and aspects that impact success. A comprehensive strategy helps make better use of resources and improve cooperation within a team.

Chapter 4
No one could possibly have seen that coming!

Why homogeneous teams and groupthink make for worse results

"Good morning!" Peter is beaming with satisfaction as he opens the meeting. "As you know, we want to discuss today, whether a slightly modified product will enable us to address new target audiences. There is a lot of potential in that!" He looks around the room full of expectation and his team members react with the nod he had hoped for.

"No undue pressure, but I met Martin at the elevator yesterday and have used that opportunity to quickly run the idea by him. Obviously, we still need to make a feasibility check, but to miss such an opportunity? He was excited by the idea and has promised to address the topic at the next board meeting." Peter was visibly proud of his coup.

"Obviously, we can't make any mistakes now. But if we put our heads together, we'll manage as a group. And even diverse perspectives are guaranteed. Yasmin, Linda, don't hold back on the female perspective!" He quickly looks at the two who manage a pained smile.

At the end of the meeting, John and Curt leave the room together with Yasmin. Peter was highly satisfied with the discussion and had left hurriedly to speak with Martin about the next steps regarding the board presentation. The others were still collecting their stuff and apparently were in no rush to return to their desks.

It is John who opens the discussion after the three had walked in silence for some time. "Well, let's just hope for the best".

"Sure" says Curt. "Nothing wrong with hoping. Never hurts."

"Seriously. Peter must be out of his mind! Now something quickly cobbled together. After all, it is not as if we hadn't tried something like that before."

Yasmin, who is quite new to the team, looks at the two in surprise. "What do you mean?"

"Obviously, the topic hasn't come up for the first time. But each time we find out that a few simple modifications are not sufficient. And I don't even want to think about the interface with production."

"Exactly", Curt nods.

"So why didn't you say anything?"

Even with his short welcome, Peter has managed to reduce the probability that any serious new insights would be gained in that meeting to a bare minimum. He clearly missed his goal of identifying any potential stumbling blocks that might threaten the project's success. We'll take a closer look at three aspects in this chapter. Why diverse teams achieve better results, why groupthink reduced the potential of homogeneous teams and priming.

Priming

Many of you have probably already used → *priming* to prepare a decision. Since a remark at the right moment to the right people can create interest or excitement, priming is a common approach in stakeholder management. In such cases, a "prime" is a measure that is deployed to influence an occurrence further down the line. Just as Peter wanted to interest Martin in the new solution to make sure he would promote the topic with the board.

That is exactly what the priming effect is about, a commonly used tool in marketing. A product or a service is depicted in a way that creates positive associations to influence the target audience. That way, the presentation of a product suggests that it is particularly healthy, or a financial advisor especially trustworthy.

We also prime in everyday interactions, though we are not necessarily aware of it. Often, we unintentionally create associations that don't support our intentions and earn reactions that we hadn't expected.

All meeting participants are fully aware of Peter's excitement and keep concerns to themselves that could endanger the board presentation. Additionally, Peter specifically asked Yasmin and Linda for different views, giving the male team members an easy excuse to lean back and avoid any danger of making themselves unpopular with unwanted reservations.

It is not sufficient, though, to just avoid this kind of rather obvious blunder. Our brain is great at also picking up messages that are way more subtle. Terms like "putting our heads together" and "as a group" create associations of harmony. As a result, people can be incited to keep any critical or contrary views to themselves.

The Florida effect is a powerful illustration of priming: In an experiment conducted at New York University, two groups of students were asked to form short sentences from lists of five words. One group of subjects was given random words. The other had words that tend to be associated with old age, like "forgetful", "bald", "gray" and "Florida". After the exercise, participants were asked to walk down a short corridor to another room to fill out a form. Researchers timed the walk, and found that people who had worked with the list of words associated with old age walked more slowly than the others. This was despite the fact that none of them said in an interview that they felt old or had recognized a theme in the words on their list.[54]

This effect also works the other way around. After test subjects had been unobtrusively induced to spend some time moving in a slow manner perceived as typical of elderly people, they ascribed more elderly-stereotypic characteristics to a subject than did their peers.[55]

Groupthink

There is another aspect that makes groups fall silent and helps answer Yasmin's question as to why no one voiced their concerns: →*groupthink*. This term describes a behaviour that is especially common in homogenous teams. It means that differing opinions are not addressed or contrary ideas shared by their members. Instead →*Conformity* develops. Even if people disagree with what is being said or decided, they don't speak up out of fear to disturb the harmony and cohesion of the group. They censor themselves to fit in seamlessly.

One of the earliest experiments to demonstrate that effect was conducted by Solomon Asch in the 1960s. Subjects were shown pictures with four lines and were asked to identify those that were of the same length (see figure 5). Not really a difficult exercise. Questioned by themselves, 95 percent gave the correct answer.

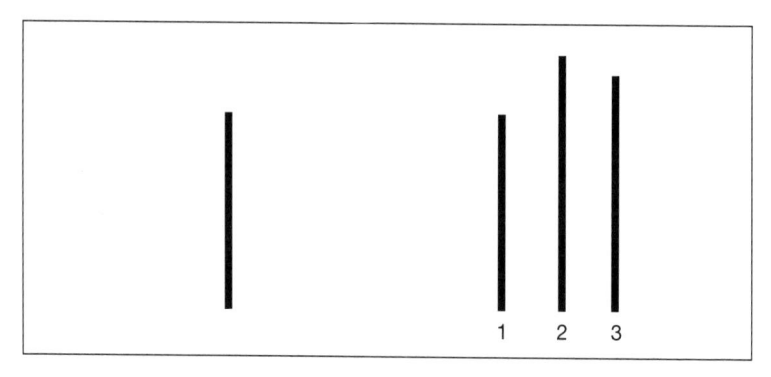

Figure 5: Asch conformity experiment

This looked very different when subjects were interviewed as part of a group. The other members were all part of the set-up of the experiment. They gave mostly incorrect answers, and apparently all agreed. All gave their assessments one after the other, with the subjects being among the last to speak. This way, they found themselves confronted with a group of people united in their false judgement. This had an impact. Usually teh subject followed the majority vote against their better knowledge. Almost three quarters provided answers that were obviously wrong.

One of the reasons why people follow the majority vote despite their better judgement can be visualized today, thanks to modern medical imaging technology. People have always relied on others for their survival. If one fell out of line or was excluded from the tribe, they were in immediate danger. Consequently, the feeling of being rejected activates the same brain regions as physical pain.[56]

We do not even realize what we are missing

Often, those involved do not even realize that group dynamic processes can hide important information. Today, the catastrophic reactor accident at Chernobyl is considered a classic example of the dangers of groupthink. The immediate reason for the disaster was not technical malfunction but a series of wrong decisions. The staff at that time were a knowledgeable and highly experienced team that should have been able to bring the situation under control. But their very experience created a false sense of security. They ignored regulations and instead relied on their own assessment. Any concerns were rationalized or not even addressed, to avoid appearing to be an outsider. They were the experts, insecurity would be perceived as weakness, and worriers or weaklings should not interfere.[57]

Luckily, the consequences of groupthink are not quite as dramatic in most teams. Nonetheless, it can have a strong negative impact on the quality of decisions and prevent teams from leveraging the knowledge and experience of team members.

In many cases, those involved are completely unaware that they remain well below their potential. On the contrary, the fact that everyone is quick to agree is often seen as an indicator of the quality of the work. As nobody questions the outcomes, group members do not even consider the possibility that they could be wrong. Diverse teams, on the other hand, that ponder different alternatives, compete for the best solution and fight over the best approach, are highly aware of the different alternatives. That is why they are less satisfied and more unsure about the quality of their work, even if they arrive at better solutions.[58]

For this reason – other than what one might expect – a great team climate does not necessarily guarantee exceptional results and does not automatically ensure that everyone freely speaks their mind and shares opposing ideas. Instead, an easy and friendly collaboration can be the perfect breeding ground for groupthink, because everyone believes they are in agreement anyway, and conflict would be especially painful.

Providing space for different perspectives

It is worthwhile to actively use methods that help reduce groupthink in order to make different ideas visible. That is especially true in teams that are relatively homogenous.

When strong team members take a clear stand at the beginning of a discussion, others are more likely to hold back with differing views. That's why it is helpful if they restrain themselves initially and let others talk first. It can also be instructive to take an opposing view initially and see how things develop. This is the basis for the "Six Thinking Hats" by Edward de Bono. In that exercise, each participant takes a clear stand that is defined by the color of their hat (see table 6). Such a clear indication that critical questions are not just accepted but actively desired is often needed to show team members they have permission to share their perspectives and concerns.

Color	Perspective	Role
White	Objective, neutral, and unbiased point of view	Looks for concrete facts, no interpretations or opinions

Red	Subjective, emotional thinking	Personal view, passionate and emotional, including positive and negative emotions. Contradictions are possible.
Black	Logical, negative thinking	Focused on objective arguments that highlight negative aspects and potential risks. Often based on past experience.
Yellow	Realistic optimism	Constructive and optimistic but always ruled by logic. Looks at opportunities and benefits.
Green	Innovation, creativity and association	New, original ideas, crossing boundaries, and making the impossible possible.
Blue	Structured thought	Structures ideas and thoughts, pointing out alternatives, suggesting new strategies, and maintaining control. Keeps the group from getting distracted or stuck.

Table 6: The "Six Thinking Hats" according to Edward de Bono

Usually it helps to start discussions by giving everyone the time to consider their views and insights on the subject before sharing their ideas with the full group. This not only allows quieter, more reflective or introverted participants to first sort their thoughts before others press ahead. It also helps prevent missing out on important thoughts because the discussion quickly develops in one direction and it doesn't seem worth any more to bring them up.

Especially with touchy subjects it is a good idea, to discuss them in twos or small groups first, before sharing outcomes with the full team. Most people feel more comfortable sharing their concerns in a smaller circle. Having voiced them once – and maybe even getting support – provides the necessary safety to stand up to a bigger audience.

Diverse teams are more innovative

These methods help to reduce groupthink and bring up different perspectives in teams that are relatively homogenous. After all, people who appear to have a lot in common – due to their gender, race or age

– probably still have different experiences that impact their views. A single woman living in a fancy apartment and just settling into a new town most certainly lives a different life from the woman who provides for a family with two children and who has been living in a house in the suburbs for years.

According to research conducted by Boston Consulting Group and the Technical University Munich, four factors mostly increase innovation. Two of them – experience in different industries and career paths – have nothing to do with the usual focus areas of companies' diversity efforts. Teams that also include people of different genders and from different countries have more marketable ideas and achieve a bigger share of their revenues with new products and solutions.[59]

A similar effect was discovered in a broad survey that looked at the impact that national and cultural diversity in Greater London had on the economy. Based on data from over 7,500 businesses, researchers found that companies – independent of type – achieve a "diversity bonus". Those with a diverse leadership team introduced more innovative products than their homogeneous competitors. They were better able to attract international clients and to prosper in the multi-cultural London environment.[60]

The British Center for Talent Innovation (CTI) has identified some of the reasons: On the one hand, the probability of developing solutions that are meaningful for a target group increases significantly if at least one team members shares key demographics with that audience. Also, more than half of the leaders don't support ideas that don't resonate with them personally and for which they see no need. People lacking the experience or mental flexibility to understand that other people need different things from them block innovation. That's why both inherent diversity and acquired diversity – aspects such as cultural fluency, generational savvy, cross-functional knowledge, global mindset, language skills – impact the quality of a team and its decisions.[61]

There are increasingly voices that highlight the fact that diversity is not about creating more and more "colorful" teams. That the goal must be different perspectives, that is, diversity of thought. Everyone merely relying on acquired diversity is missing out, though. Study after study shows that visible or innate differences increase performance.

The positive impact of women and men working together has long been proven. The German Stock Exchange is currently experimenting with a diversity index. Out of the 100 biggest public listed companies in Germany, the "Diversity DAX" consists of the 30 companies that are ranked the highest in terms of gender equity for the executive and supervisory board. In a two year span, this experimental index has outperformed the regular one by about 4.3 percentage points.[62]

The Credit Suisse Research Institute found out that companies with 25 percent women on their management teams have a four percent higher cash flow yield.[63] Additionally, executive teams and supervisory boards that consist of both women and men ensure better corporate governance. Based on the survey of 2,500 companies over a period of six years, they also found that those with at least one woman on their top team have reaped higher returns and bigger growth. Simply put: for shareholders it would on average have been smarter to invest in companies with female top leaders than without.

Looking for the reasons for the phenomenon, the institute dug deep into the existing research. That's when they found that the success had nothing to do with superior skills or insights of individual contributors. Instead, everyone showed a better performance on a diverse team, because additional perspectives were being considered and discussed. Also, one very human aspect had a strong positive impact: participants prepared better because they were more afraid of embarrassing themselves in front of people different from themselves.[64]

An experiment carried out in the US shows that lack of diversity can literally be deadly. It explored the impact of jurors' skin-color on the probability of a fair trial. An all-white jury versus one with white and black members had to determine whether a black suspect was guilty. If it was a mixed jury, the probability that the defendant was deemed guilty before the start of the deliberation decreased. The researchers identified a cause that also shows up in other studies: just knowing that they were going to be part of a mixed jury was sufficient to make participants consider the biases they might have and how they could impact their decision. Also, they were more careful with hasty judgements. The same effect became visible during the discussion. In mixed juries the debates took longer, considerably more facts were discussed and participants made fewer false statements regarding the case.[65]

Tips for diverse perspectives

Support your intentions with a smart selection of words. What we say has a big impact beyond the statements we make and the intentions we have. Someone looking for a constructive dialog that surfaces different ideas and perspectives should invite participants to have a "lively discussion" or "critical debate" rather than highlighting commonalities and team spirit.

Provide space for different perspectives. In a discussion, give time for individual reflection. Make use of cards or post-its to collect a wide range of ideas. Create psychological safety, e.g. by having participants act according to pre-defined roles or having small group discussions.

Invite people to "dare". It is easier to voice a contradictory idea if someone else does, too, even if it is different from one's own. Visibly demonstrate that you welcome other thoughts and stop any attempts on the part of the majority to interrupt or silence team members with a differing perspective. Ask actively for critical feedback and show that you value those insights.

Avoid echo chambers that only resound your own view. Don't rely on your closest confidants if you have to make a difficult decision. Talk to people who have completely different suggestions and make sure to understand why.

Diversify your environment. Make sure that your team, your friends and acquaintances and your network also include people with different roots and perspectives. Try new things, whether they are foreign countries, cuisines, or literature. Seek new experiences and exchanges even if they make you feel uncomfortable (initially).

Chapter 5

You always do that exceptionally well!

Why delegation is often unfair and thwarts employees

Monday morning, 9:00 a.m.. "I hope you had a nice and relaxing weekend and just can't wait to get back to work!" Peter welcomes his team with the usual enthusiasm to their weekly meeting.

While people are still signaling their agreement, he continues. "Over the last weeks, we have been heavily engaged in the board presentation. Obviously, that can't hurt our other work. That's why I have asked Alexander to take the lead on the work for the executive team." He smiles at his team member, who beams back proudly. "Thanks for doing that! I know we can rely on you."

"For the rest of us, it means back to basics. Let's get ourselves an overview first. Linda, would you take the minutes?"

"That doesn't fit well today. Actually, I took them for the last two meetings, already."

"I know, I know! Your minutes are always exemplary. You do that especially well! And even if it is tight at times, all of us have to take on duties on top of our daily business. Look at Alex – a true team player!"

Most of us have probably experienced it already: unpopular tasks tend to be distributed unevenly and that's completely independent of skills or qualifications. They are described as "office housework" in the literature and women tend to get stuck with them – also outside their own homes – or they are delegated to people whose skin color isn't white.

Unpopular tasks are distributed unfairly

Whether minutes are to be written or lists kept up to date, whether it's about booking a conference room or cleaning it up afterwards, ordering lunch or getting some birthday present: nearly one woman in three says that such tasks predominantly land at her feet.[66] The same is true with onboarding new staff or taking care of colleagues who are unwell or having difficulties – "He currently has issues with his wife. Could you talk to him?" – which are predominately delegated to women, regardless of industry. While these tasks are undoubtedly important and enable the functioning of a department, they have one thing in common: they are neither glamorous nor recommend anyone for promotion.

Personality and style also influence the tasks that land on our desks. Western culture has fully embraced the Greco-Roman ideal of the great rhetorician. People who have poise and speak with authority are in the perfect position for exciting assignments and higher honors. We value action over contemplation, which means we often put less trust in people who prefer to stay in the background. While highly charismatic employees get the chance to impact strategic projects, introverts and their contribution are often overlooked and undervalued.[67]

Organizations don't do themselves any favors this way. Both extraversion and introversion have distinct strengths that can come to play in different situations. While extroverts often can inspire and enthrall others, their actions are influenced by the fact that appreciation and positive feedback clearly matter to them. Also, they are impulsive and easier to distract, and pay less attention to details. That's why apparently unimportant details can easily be pushed aside, trusting in the right gut feeling instead. That can lead to (too) quick decisions or premature actions, which is not without danger when making strategic decisions.

Their need for security makes introverts skeptical about quick solutions. While they can lose themselves in the myriads of data they encounter in everyday life, they also have the ability to pursue a topic even against resistance and not to give up if initial results prove frustrating. As they are less reliant on the perception of others and less receptive to rewards, they can better distance themselves from the opinions and attitudes of their environment. This creates independence and enables them to think "outside the box".[68]

Also, younger employees complain of boredom. Although almost 90 percent of millennials want to develop and grow their careers, not even 40 percent have the impression that they've learned anything new in the last 30 days.[69]

The fact that women and members of (ethnic) minorities are often stuck with tasks that "simply have to be done" is strongly connected to stereotypes, biases and preconceived expectations as to who has which strengths, interests and responsibilities – as a member of a group rather than an individual. Women are supposed to be friendly and supportive and not push for attention. They are expected to be engaged team players who put the interests of the company and their team above their own ambitions.[70] The same holds true for people of color, who are more often expected to take on supportive roles in the office. After all, such expectations are aligned with our daily experience and the roles in which they are still often depicted in the movies.[71]

And another aspect has an impact: people who are confronted with stereotypical expectations are less likely to say "no" to unpopular tasks.[72] That makes it easier for those who ask, because they are unlikely to end up with any unpleasant discussions. At the same time it reinforces the status quo.

Resistance is futile

Pushing back often is not a great option however. Whether through open opposition or clandestine boycott by means of turning in poor work, strategies that usually work well for others and ensure they are never asked again, can easily backfire for women and minorities. Not meeting expectations often results in punishment.[73] "She thinks she is too good for that" or "he is holding back the team", they say. Payback follows immediately – or at the next performance evaluation.

But an unfair distribution of tasks hurts the team beyond the consequences individuals have to bear, because it impacts the group cohesion and creates unnecessary friction. Because people who take minutes are less likely to fully engage in the discussion and interesting perspectives will be missed. And because they might simply give up eventually and leave the company or at least the department.

If you are kept busy with administrative tasks, you hardly have the time or opportunity to take on activities that broaden your experience, create visibility and support your career, like strategic projects, or joining a committee that provides the opportunity to make new contacts and build new relationships. Also, presentations or lectures offer the chance to strengthen one's own image or that of the firm. Women as well as people of color or a migration background are often overlooked if such opportunities arise.[74]

This has fatal consequences for those concerned. While functional competencies and a good track record are key to success in a leadership role, it is something else that actually gets you there: visibility. To be seen and known is the key factor that helps people make it to the top.[75]

To explain an unequal distribution of tasks, lack of interest or lack of confidence are often mentioned. A major research study that followed the careers of 3,500 MBA students after graduation shows this is not true. Women and men pursued very similar strategies to advance their careers, but it paid off much more for men. Especially among those who kept open all options for advancement – whether internally or at a different firm – male graduates advanced way faster than their female peers. Almost twice as many made it to the top over the same period.[76]

An underdeveloped skill

Despite its huge importance, delegation is an underdeveloped skill that gets little attention and is rarely used deliberately. While nearly one in two companies have doubts that their managers know how to do it well, only about one in four actually takes action to change that.[77] But smart delegation is not just important to make sure a team achieves its goals. It is also a prerequisite for all members to have a chance to develop and build critical skills, learn something new, stay engaged and motivated. At the same time it allows leaders to tackle activities beyond the daily business, like building new relationships and strengthening collaboration with other departments.

In the end, it is not just women and minorities who benefit if tasks are distributed fairly. Also, introverted (white) men who don't immediately raise their hand to apply for an interesting task, have better chances to take on new responsibilities. The same holds true for anyone who avoids shining the spotlight onto themselves. It even benefits the extraverted, highly engaged "star" of a department who might believe that saying no will hurt their career or – even worse – that everything will fall to pieces if they don't volunteer.

Routine tasks

How to delegate everyday responsibilities in a fair and equal manner?

- **Get an overview:** Consider the tasks that must be managed on a regular basis, and how often they are due. It usually helps to conduct a short survey of your team members. Often that also provides first insights into the distribution of tasks and whether it is fair.
- **Use a system:** Whether people take on recurring tasks in alphabetical order, chronologically or following any other rule, a structured approach helps to ensure that standard tasks are distributed fairly.

- **Don't rely on volunteers:** Otherwise stereotypes and social pressure will ensure that the usual suspects will be stuck with the lion's share of unpopular tasks – whether they like it or not. Even distributing tasks according to preferences – whether true or assumed – tends to lead to an unequal distribution across the team, with women probably taking care of birthday cakes and flowers, while others shine with functional expertise.
- **Be consistent:** It is a matter of course that everyone on the team executes the tasks assigned to them, however unpopular. "I am not that much into details" or "that is not really my thing" are not excuses but bad behaviour and poor performance.

Visible projects

In order to staff high visibility projects it's not enough just to rely on gut feeling. Instead it is essential to identify criteria that are critical to success and take it from there. Although there is a broader range of factors that impact decision-making, one still needs to ensure that everyone gets their chance to shine.[78]

- **Get an overview.** Create a list of priorities and upcoming tasks and the skills required to manage them successfully.
- **Identify owners.** Consider which team members can take on which responsibilities. If you are unsure whether they have got what it takes, question your own feelings. You might discover some of the biases, prejudices and reservations you have. If in doubt, get a second opinion.
- **Enable growth.** If your selection is limited due to project requirements, there could still be an opportunity to ask a more junior team member to join together with an "old hand" and gain relevant experience.
- **Keep track of your options.** Create a table that includes relevant information about team members and helps you recognize opportunities as they arise. This should include your own observations,

feedback from others, information about their goals and preferences that they have shared with you. What motivates or frustrates them?
- **Plan for development, not just during performance reviews.** Add to your notes, whenever you have ideas about development opportunities that can support people's careers. What tasks would be meaningful? Who else should they meet?

While creating such an overview requires some effort initially, it is easy to keep up to date. Just 15 minutes per week are sufficient to provide you with an invaluable tool to live up to the needs of very different team members.

Delegating fairly

To enable one's team members to develop, it is not enough to simply drop a project into someone's lap and micro-manage afterwards out of fear that something might go wrong, or to pass the buck and pray everything goes well, or that the person now in charge reaches out in time before things go downhill.

A few measures considerably increase the probability of everything going well and the expected outcomes being achieved:

- **Good preparation is a prerequisite for success.** If role, content, basic parameters and expectations are unclear, disappointment is almost guaranteed. That's why it is important to agree up front about goals and timing and to think about the challenges that are likely to occur during the course of a project.
- **No "by the way" or "before I forget" delegation.** Take sufficient time to discuss the project in a structured manner. Why you have asked them to take on a specific task, what thinking has led to that decision, what are the requirements and your expectations? Come to an agreement regarding outcomes, timing as well as milestones. As you are not just delegating work but responsibility, this has to be

a dialog – as opposed to a monologue – to align the notions of all concerned.
- **Be perfectly clear on importance and responsibility.** Often people don't take enough time to make sure that project owners are fully on board and realize the scope of their commitment. That they are clear on expected results, their role, the need to drive the project consistently as well as consequences for the team and the organization if they fail to deliver.
- **Conclude comprehensive agreements.** The aim of this discussion is to come to a joint agreement of what is to be done by when and why. It requires the employee to repeat in her or his own words what has been agreed and the next steps they will take. Simply asking "All clear?" and getting a "yes" can easily hide the fact that all may in truth be far from clear. Using an approach that ensures that any open issues are really addressed is especially important in diverse teams. Aspects like cultural and social expectations could stop members from admitting any uncertainties. Alternatively, less experienced team members might simply be unaware that they are missing important information.
- **Tell key stakeholders.** It is insufficient if only the project owners know what they are supposed to do. Important stakeholders must also be informed about their role and what it entails.

If there are any issues during the course of a project, they should be considered as development opportunities. Rather than taking charge themselves, leaders should coach the project owner through the process to help them develop the required knowledge and effective solutions. In order to avoid unpleasant surprises and any emergencies, regular updates are required.[79]

Tips for fair delegation

Rotate unpopular tasks. Get yourself an overview of "office housework" regularly due in your team. Use a structured approach – chronologically or by alphabet – to ensure that unpopular tasks don't always end up with the same people.

Give everyone the opportunity to shine. Don't always delegate highly visible tasks to those who come to mind first. Consider the skills and experiences necessary, who meets the requirements and who could benefit from participating in a project.

Keep track. Create a table of who should gain what type of experience and why. Update it regularly.

Integrate delegation into existing responsibilities. Use delegation to enable team members to grow. Make use of relevant opportunities for people development plans as well as performance management.

Use your influence to change the norms. Point out if you see that tasks are being delegated unfairly and make others aware of the potential consequences for both individuals and the organization.

Chapter 6

Could you quickly give me a hand?

Why successful collaboration needs rules and how to address conflict

"Do you have a moment?" Curt had quickly wanted to grab a coffee before finishing the long overdue report, but Peter stopped him in his tracks, looking at him expectantly.

"Sure, no problem."

"It is because of the team offsite. You know that Yasmin's has had this great idea. Now it needs to be implemented and I've been thinking about you."

"Yeah, happy to help. What is it actually about? What do you need?"

"Well, we haven't discussed that in any detail, yet. It's still early days. Probably best if you'd set up a meeting. Maybe you could also ask some of your colleagues. Form a project team, that wouldn't be bad. Even better, a task force. That sounds strong and engaged. Modern. Like it!"

As already covered in Chapter 4, different people offer different perspectives, help avoid groupthink and thus allow for better solutions. But that's not all. Research looking at the data of major consulting firms proved that strong collaboration – also across teams – creates the basis for new market potential, higher revenues and profit. Additionally, such projects offer a better margin.

Despite all those advantages, the people involved are often less than thrilled. After all, it tends to take time to reap the benefits. Often, it feels easier and faster to just focus on one's own tasks at hand.

Thinking that way means missing the long term rewards, though, including personal advantages. These include higher visibility – also towards top management – as well as higher revenues within one's own field. After all, working closely with others also provides an opportunity to demonstrate one's expertise and skills as well as building trust. This often forms the basis for future recommendations by colleagues, if the opportunity arises.[80]

But while many of us understand intellectually that it is worthwhile to leverage each other's knowledge, experience and support, there are also potential concerns that can block cooperation. It often feels inefficient, as if everything is taking way too long. Also, it can be risky to share one's own expertise if there is a danger of being taken advantage of, if we are concerned we might be working with someone who uses our insights without recognizing our contribution, or if we simply believe it is a waste of time.

Accordingly, it can hardly come as a surprise that a culture that celebrates rock stars and rewards their behaviour is hardly a breeding ground for trusting collaboration. An inclusive environment on the other hand supports the willingness to help each other. This requires a climate where employees feel valued. Where commonalities are recognized while everyone is able to preserve their individuality within the team. Such a climate supports innovation, more intelligent and efficient solutions, and increases the performance of a group.[81]

Still it is always worthwhile to make conscious decisions about when and how to collaborate. Failing to do so can build frustration within a team or rather its members.

Way too much of a good thing

Today, people spend up to 80 percent of their time interacting with others, whether in meetings, on the phone, or responding to email. That leaves little room for one's (other) responsibilities or just to follow up on the actions from the last encounter. Performance suffers from a never-ending flow of activities and requests and even taking work home rarely helps to get everything done. This results in stress, burnout and team members giving up and leaving the company.[82]

Taking the time to analyze who collaborates with whom and the individual contributions often uncovers some surprises. Many leaders are not even aware who delivers the most support and input within their team. Network analysis regularly shows that there is no direct link between personal visibility, excessive name-dropping and an apparently unlimited number of connections and the actual impact someone has.

There can be many reasons for this. Team members might belong to a culture where it is unusual or even inappropriate to shine the light on oneself. Maybe they are simply working in the wrong place – from their home office, for example, or just a different location – and don't have the opportunity to casually highlight their success over lunch or over a beer at an after-work gathering. Also, it might just not be their style to blow their own trumpet.

There may also be a very different reason, though: that someone delivers below standard in their own job, due to the many extra tasks they have taken on. This can result in their manager losing trust in their abilities because tasks don't get done in time or at all.

Contributions vary

To better understand what is going on, it helps to take a closer look at the way that people can provide support and contribute to successful outcomes. In principle, there are three options:

1. I can deliver information, share my knowledge and expertise.
2. I offer social resources, which means creating visibility and connecting people.
3. Finally, I can provide hands-on support and invest my time and energy.

These contributions don't only differ from a "content" perspective. Even more important in this context is that, while I can quickly provide some information or make a connection, it does not work the same way with personal contributions. Usually, they take time. And while I can give the same piece of information over and over again and leverage the same contact whenever needed, time once invested is gone. And it might be lacking for my own responsibilities.

That is one of the reasons why research finds that only about half the people who are considered to be among the most helpful contacts are also recognized as high-performing employees. Colleagues that invest a lot of time and energy to help out might be a sought-after resource and highly appreciated by their peers, but they are not necessarily valued by their manager. It is others that win the laurels: about every fifth "star" of a team or an organization focusses on their own job only and doesn't even consider supporting others.[83]

In the longer term, this might not be the smartest strategy, though. "Takers" who put their own interests above those of others can be extremely successful while working independently, or as long as they manage to take advantage of the people they know. In an environment, where people need to rely on each other, where they depend on smooth collaboration that continues over time – which is virtually everywhere today – "givers" will be more successful in the medium run. These are people who help others and enable them to succeed while at the same time benefiting from their network and its support.[84]

Different behaviors and standards

But not all givers are highly successful. Employees with the lowest productivity tend to be givers, too, because they are too supportive of others. If that makes you think of women first and foremost, sadly enough you are right. While men predominantly offer support by providing information or connections, women are considerably more likely (66 percent) to offer hands-on help and invest more time and energy.[85] There are several reasons that explain their behaviour: first, women generally are more likely to act as "good citizens". One indicator? Simply looking at prisons. In Germany for example, about 3,100 women are serving a sentence at the time of writing – compared to 51,000 men. Additionally, the seriousness of the crime and sentence tend to be lower for women.[86]

Being on the outside is not the only reason that women are more likely to support their communities. Also, they have a fundamentally different view of what it means to be a team player. For them it is about helping others to get their work done. Men say that "being a good team player is knowing your position and playing it well".[87]

That helps explain why women, who are prone to feel selfish or guilty if they do, make less time to drive their own priorities.[88] Alternatively, they give up that time to support others asking for help. Rather than being appreciated, this can actually result in being perceived as less in control, on top of things and prepared.

Anyone thinking that this is simply "their problem" is half right at best. Thanks to stereotypical expectations, women's help is taken for granted. Men who – for example – stay longer at work to support a colleague are judged considerably more positively for demonstrating that behavior than a female peer. And if they go home instead, it is accepted as normal. If women do the very same thing, they are judged much more harshly.[89]

Gender is not the only aspect, though, that impacts collaboration. The ethnic make-up of a group also has a big impact. While there is plenty of proof of the strength of teams that include people of different ethnicities – they digest more information and make more qualified decisions[90], they make more reliable forecasts because they don't blindly trust each other[91], everyone tries harder, considers new ideas and delivers a better performance[92] – they are often watched with suspicion.

One experiment had observers assess what was happening in ethnically homogeneous versus mixed groups. Regardless of what was actually going on, they firmly believed that there was more friction in heterogenous teams. Groups that consisted of members of just one ethnicity were perceived as equally harmonious. In any mixed teams conflict was assumed. In their perception, this was not about the actual subject matter. Instead they thought they saw clear signals of interpersonal issues. As a consequence, there was less willingness to equip a mixed team with the financial resources required for it to successfully deliver.[93] Thus, the – unfair – negative judgement could easily become a self-fulfilling prophecy.

This was also demonstrated by a study conducted at a supermarket: researchers used metrics — how fast cashiers scan items, how much time they spend between customers, the number of absences — to track their performance. Due to the setting, they were able to measure the results of the same workers while different managers were on duty. They found that employees belonging to a minority group performed much worse under biased managers. They did not even need to believe that these managers actually disliked them or treated them poorly. Instead, there was simply less interaction between biased managers and minority employees, resulting in poorer outcomes. This can result in a vicious circle: where managers believe that minority workers are worse employees, that bias can result in poorer performance by the affected minorities, and so managers convince themselves that the minority workers indeed are worse employees.[94]

Supporting successful collaboration

There are some ground rules that help create a setting for successful collaboration with everyone contributing fairly. Such consistent standards are especially important in diverse teams with very different people working together. Failing to do so can endanger success, since personal style or national cultures can prevent members from asking relevant question or addressing open issues, because gender stereotypes can impact expectations, or due to staff working remotely setting the wrong priorities, because there is insufficient clarity about the task at hand.

- **Define requirements.** For each project, define which skills and experiences are required for success. This creates the basis on which to nominate team members and define expectations.
- **Delegate the power of decision-making.** A lot of time can be saved if decision are being taken were the action is. Agreeing early on what

project members can decide and what needs to be discussed increases the satisfaction of all involved and speeds up the process. Nowadays, there are many technical solutions that support collaboration without people being in the same place or working on something at the same time. While many organizations still rely on people "looking each other in the eye" for ultimate commitment, it is high time to question that practice.

- **Clarify goals and scope.** Agree on what to achieve and the actual scope of a project. This also includes identifying mechanisms to ensure a fair distribution of tasks – and to track whether everyone is delivering as agreed.
- **Provide Resources.** Consider and provide the (financial) resources required for success.
- **Help draw boundaries.** Different expectations often force people to take on roles they are not comfortable with. Make sure everyone knows that it is OK and even important to say "no" at times. That the team benefits if they focus on the tasks agreed. This also means walking the talk and refraining from always delegating tasks to the usual suspects – see Chapter 5.

Feedback and difficult conversations

A prerequisite to truly making this work is an environment that is open to (critical) feedback. This enables the most active volunteers to draw boundaries and also helps to address those colleagues, who are prone to forgetting about delivering on unwelcome tasks. Having a common framework and using it regularly helps establish a feedback culture in which addressing issues and concerns is normal.

To that end, it is worthwhile to agree on a feedback model as a team. This helps members to speak up without putting anyone on the defensive (see table 7; more tips regarding development oriented feedback can be found in Chapter 9).

Situation	Describe the situation. Be as specific as possible about what happened where and when.
Behaviour	Describe the behavior you have observed. Remember: you can't know what the other person intended.
Impact	Describe your reaction to that behavior. What you have thought and / or felt,

Table 7: An agreed model makes giving feedback easier

Feedback helps clarify a situation and hopefully results in an apology: "I am sorry, that was not my intention. I'll be more careful in the future". Still, things can turn out very unlike how they were planned. That often happens if both sides have a very different perspective on the matter at hand and insist that their view is correct. In that case, the outcome might not be going for a cup of coffee but a (smoldering) conflict.

One reason can be different personality styles: while introverts, for example, like to retreat in difficult situations and avoid conflict, extroverts are likely to follow a very different strategy. They prefer to go on the offensive. While their attempt to resolve the situation can clear the air, the consequences can also be quite different. In that case their counterpart is offended and hurt, and the exchange becomes limited to attack and defense.[95]

Also, both parties have something at stake. We had an agreement and the other did not deliver. I exposed myself by trusting someone and was let down. I made a great contribution that was ignored or – even worse – someone else stole my laurels. A colleague irritates me no end or just gets on my nerves. Someone gave me feedback that I consider unfair.

When emotions are involved, matters get no easier. The "normal reaction" is to postpone that discussion. Alternatively, we try to address the "matter" while keeping our feelings out of it. Both strategies are unlikely to succeed, because on the inside, it keeps rumbling.

Truly resolving such an issue needs a different approach. After all, what keeps boiling on the inside is a mixture of my view of the situation and the resulting emotions, all of which are potentially in conflict with my self-image. After all, I might have to recognize that I have a bias I was not aware of, or to accept that I am not quite as fair, friendly and helpful as I like to believe.

That's why the basis for a constructive dialog is to recognize that our own view of the situation is not the only one possible. That our expectations, experiences and evaluation impact our judgement of what is going on. Accordingly, it is really not just one dialog taking place, it is actually three different conversations that are needed to enable us to agree on what has happened and what it resulted in (see table 8). Thus, a "battle of messages" can be avoided, creating space for a "learning conversation", that serves everyone involved.[96]

	A Battle of Messages	A Learning Conversation
The "What Happened?" Conversation Challenge: The situation is more complex than either person can see.	Assumption: I know all I need to know to understand what happened.	Assumption: Each of us is bringing different information and perceptions to the table: there are likely to be important things that each of us doesn't know.
	Goal: Persuade them I am right.	Goal: Explore each other's stories: how we understand the situation and why.
	Assumption: I know what they intended.	Assumption: I know what I intended, and the impact their actions had on me. I don't and can't know what's in their head.
	Goal: Let them know what they did is wrong.	Goal: Share the impact on me, and find out what they were thinking. Also find out what impact I'm having on them.
	Assumption: It's all their fault. (Or it's all my fault.)	Assumption: We have probably *both* contributed to this mess.
	Goal: Get them to admit blame and take responsibility for making amends.	Goal: Understand the contribution system: how our actions interact to produce this result.
The Feelings Conversation Challange: The situation is emotionally charged.	Assumption: Feelings are irrelevant and wouldn't be helpful to share. (Or, my feelings are their fault and they need to hear about them.)	Assumption: Feelings are the heart of the situation Feelings are usually complex. I may have to dig a bit to understand my feelings.
	Goal: Avoid talking about feelings. (Or, let'em have it!)	Goal: Address feelings (mine and theirs) without judgement or attributions. Acknowledge feelings before problem solving.

The Identity Conversation Challenge: The situation threatens our identity.	Assumption: I'm competent or incompetent, good or bad, loveable or unlovable. There is no in-between.	Assumption: There may be a lot at stake psychologically for both of us. Each of us is complex, neither of us perfect.
	Goal: Protect my all-or-nothing self-image.	Goal: Understand the identity issue on the line for both of us. Build a more complex self-image to maintain my balance better.

Table 8: Learning conversation instead of "war of messages", Douglas Stone, Bruce Patton and Sheila Heen, *Difficult Conversations*.

Tips for better collaboration

In your mind, review the meetings you conduct. Consider whether all of them are really necessary, whether all participants need to be invited and have something to contribute. Plan for shorter meetings and consider stand-up sessions to keep them brief and increase discipline.

Get to know key helpers. Which team members spend above average time on tasks outside their own area of responsibility? Is that intentional and does it make sense? Is it being rewarded appropriately? Alternatively, are they taking on too much and do they need help to set boundaries and focus on priorities?

Establish fair and efficient standards for projects. Keep team size reasonable based on what is needed. Select members based on the skills and experience required for success as well as learning opportunities provided. Give people accountability – including the power to make decisions.

Make feedback part of your team culture. Leverage established practices to make sure that feedback – also critical – becomes an everyday occurrence.

> **Practice difficult conversations.** Accept that it is really three conversations taking place: what has happened, how did it make me feel and what does the situation say about me? Reach out even if you have not yet come to terms with your own contribution to the issue at hand. Continuing your inner dialog means speculating – perhaps completely off the mark – and missing out on an opportunity to find a constructive solution.

PART 3
GETTING IN AND UP

The following chapters are focused on careers and the factors that impact who is being hired and promoted. After all, personal demographics massively impact our opportunities on the labor market as well as the likeliness and speed of advancement.

Chapter 7, *"I know the perfect candidate!"*, examines how people get a job. Who learns about an open position, who is being addressed as part of the hiring process? What are the criteria that impact the probability of someone actually being selected? It also shows how a fair and smart selection can be ensured.

Chapter 8, *"He doesn't look the role!"*, highlights the factors beyond qualification that impact whether or not someone is considered for a larger role. The mechanisms that quicken some careers and slow down or even block others. Finally, it provides help to create a level playing field.

Chapter 9, *"I didn't yet have a chance to provide feedback"*, explores the fundamental differences that exist in whether, when and what kind of feedback someone gets.

Chapter 7

I know the perfect candidate!

How we exclude people during the application process

"I know the perfect candidate for the job!", Yasmin looks at Peter expectantly. "He is fabulous. Engaged, flexible. Currently working for a non-profit organization. He has done this extremely cool project and would be able to contribute so much!"

"Well, let's first post that role and see who applies", John intervenes. "I'd strongly propose that we cast a wide net. There is currently so much change in that area. I am sure there are great profiles we are not even aware of right now."

"Seriously? You know how it is", Yasmin can hardly believe the bureaucracy of the suggested approach. "It would take ages. Endless discussions with HR. And we want to change things now!"

"But it is a chance for us to strengthen the team for the longer run. We shouldn't throw that away. Just out of convenience."

In reaction to John's appeal, Yasmin just shrugs her shoulders. "Peter, what do you think? Why don't the two of you meet for coffee? I can call him right now. I am sure he can make it work over the next few days."

Generally, more and more hiring is happening via personal connections. In Germany, this is true for one in three positions overall, and almost one in two in companies with less than 50 employees.[97] While such an approach might appear convenient and very efficient – after all, it should be fast and there is probably a great fit as people come with relevant recommendations – it can create barriers for job seekers. As we know from Chapter 3, most networks are homogeneous. Depending on ambitions, people who are not part of the mainstream are often less likely to have the "right" contacts and meaningful relationships that can help them land their dream job.

It is not just potential applicants, though, who pay the price for this approach. The same is true for organizations. They are missing out on interesting candidates and great talents outside their radar, who could offer new insights and perspectives. Instead the current approach can easily increase groupthink and decrease competitiveness.

Even companies that do post all openings often fall short of their potential. One example is the British police. It knew that it would be better able to serve communities if its staff reflected the diversity of the population. But it struggled to achieve that goal, as applicants from a black or minority ethnic (BME) background were more likely to fail the online Situational Judgment Test (SJT). This multiple-choice, online assessment tests how would-be recruits might respond to real situations that officers have to face and it forms a key part of the recruitment process.

Thanks to insights from behavioral science, it was possible to improve the success rate of BME applicants without modifying the test itself. Instead, priming was used to help candidates to imagine relevant situations: as part of the email invitation, a few sentences were added. They prompted applicants to reflect on what might make them a good addition to the force, and what significance that would bear in their community. This simple intervention considerably increased the success rate for the target audience and had no effect on applicants from non-BME backgrounds. Effectively, the intervention closed the probability gap of passing the test between BMEs and non-BME applicants.[98]

Appealing – just not to everyone

Another subject, the same issue: especially for occupations with a high share of male job holders, job adverts – due to visuals and the language used – often predominantly appeal to men. It is almost impossible to make up for that at a later stage in the application process: Based on the wording of an ad one can make a pretty reliable prognosis regarding the gender of the person finally selected.[99]

In Chapter 1, I explained how girls from 6 to 12 feel less qualified for a profession if they don't feel addressed. If organizations just seek an "engineer" or a "mechanic" versus a "female or male astronaut". Grown women react differently. They have no doubts about their own qualification if a job posting does not appeal to them. If the visualization or wording are stereotypically male, they simply conclude that the job is not attractive and they would not fit with that organization. With gender-inclusive language, the company and position are evaluated more positively.[100]

Also, the list of requirements has an impact, with a long list negatively impacting the share of female applicants. One often-cited HP study finds that women only apply if they meet 100 percent of the requirements, while men do so if they can just tick 60 percent off the boxes, has become a classic. Often people conclude that women don't have enough self-confidence, that they are not "brave enough". One interesting study offers a different interpretation. It finds that women – unlike men – accept those requirements at face value. That's why they don't want to waste time applying – neither theirs nor that of others. Accordingly, the difference is not about confidence. It is about compliance and the perception of the process and the rules of the game.[101]

An experiment at Stanford University emphasized why the popular advice that "women must be more prepared to take risks" falls short. They created two fictitious resumes of applicants for a lab manager position, which varied in just one detail: the name. Over one hundred scientists at academic institutions agreed to assess the candidates and were randomly assigned the CV of either "Jennifer" or "John".

Despite the exact same wording of the resume, Jennifer was considered less qualified by both men and women. As a result, the scientists were less willing to hire and to mentor her – and they suggested a lower starting salary. On average, Jennifer was offered 13 percent less salary than John.[102]

This experiment not only demonstrates that qualifications and guts are not enough to succeed, where stereotypes and social and societal expectations are involved. It also it demonstrates that women are no "better" or "fairer" people and that mixed interview panels are insufficient to solve the issue. Women tend to be influenced by exactly the same stereotypes. They are unlikely to be any less prejudiced under the same conditions than their male colleagues. That is despite the fact that they obviously know – just like the vast majority of men – that women are no less smart, qualified or engaged. We fall for stereotypes, even if we know fully well that they are wrong.

This is not just an issue that impacts opportunities for women: "Recent examination of the role of leadership prototypes and race has consistently found a pro-white leadership bias", explains business psychologist Binna Kandola. "For white people, the bias is an in-group preference because the in-group is white. But minorities also show the same pro-white bias." The effect? "Someone with a pro-white leadership bias is likely to assume that a white leader has leadership traits – even if they have not observed these traits themselves. Any gaps or discrepancies in a person's leadership performance are filled in or explained away more favorably for a white leader than a minority one."[103]

To ensure a fair personnel selection, other measures than just telling people to dare more are required.

The starting point must be a reasonable definition of what is actually required. The common practice, to define a virtually endless list of expectations, is not a good idea. The issue is not only the inflated pool of candidates who meet a varying number and differently relevant requirements and cause unnecessary screening work. Such an approach also forms the basis for selection based on "cultural fit" – picking those people who promise to seamlessly integrate into day-to-day operations.

Selecting the people who "fit in"

Sadly, the perception of what "fits" is affected by many factors that have nothing whatsoever to do with qualification. Our first name already triggers an expectation regarding origin and skills and impact opportunities. In the US, "Emily" and "Greg" are more likely to find a job than "Lakisha" or "Jamal", names indicating that the candidate is a person of color.[104]

In Germany, the situation is similar for "Murat", with the very name impacting the grade point average. Students at a teacher training college were asked to score tests of children whose names indicated German roots versus non-German ancestors. With the same number of mistakes, "Murat" – presumably of Turkish descent – received lower scores.[105] Also, children with names like Kevin, Mandy or Chantal, who are assumed to come from families with a lower social status, tend to have fewer opportunities. As early as elementary school, teachers believe they are potential trouble. They have high expectations, on the other hand, for Sophie, Charlotte and Jakob, who are believed to be strong students and socially compatible.[106]

But if (German) teachers think that "Kevin is not a name but a diagnosis"[107], their reservations can quickly become a self-fulfilling prophecy. After all, the likelihood is high that they focus their attention on more "promising" children.

In the 1960s, Harvard Professor Robert Rosenthal created a lot of excitement when he offered a school the use of a newly developed test to evaluate the academic potential of their first- and second-graders. The principal was thrilled and immediately followed through. Based on the test, an average of 20 percent of the children showed unusual potential for intellectual growth. The names of these children were given to each teacher, who was told that their scores on the "test for intellectual blooming" indicated that they would show unusual intellectual gains during the academic year, even if there previously had been no such indication.

Eight months later, Rosenthal returned to evaluate how the pupils had developed. His result seemed to prove the quality of the test and the significance of the screening. Not just the IQ of the children identified had increased significantly more than that of others. According to their teachers, they were more curious, happier, were coping especially well and demonstrated great promise for their future development.

The only issue with the test: it was complete nonsense. The allegedly promising talents had been selected at random. What had enabled their extraordinary development was not their (bigger) potential. Instead, the way they were being treated had changed. Teachers kept more eye contact, smiled more, nodded in appreciation. Also, they called on them more often, gave more time to respond and set higher goals for these children.[108]

We knew that anyway

It's not only lack of attention that creates barriers for Kevin and Mandy. Another issue is that we are more likely to notice things that are in line with our expectations and we remember them better. This is known as → *Confirmation Bias*. If Mandy misbehaves, it shows – once more! – what we knew all along. Should Sophie behave the same way, it is an absolute exception and we are sure it will never happen again.

The fact that people are being judged based on their names has its roots in biases regarding social origins, and it is a factor that maintains low social (class) mobility. After all, not just "foreign sounding" names tell a story. Even names with a long tradition in any given country are an indicator of social class, and parents' preferences differ considerably based on aspects including education level. Accordingly, first names are an indicator of the social group that parents belong to and they have an impact on the development opportunities that are open to their children.[109]

And social mobility is decreasing. While income mobility was a reality for many people born between 1955 and 1975, it has stagnated since then. This means that children born into the bottom of the income distribution now have less chance to move up and improve their occupational status and earnings than their parents and previous generations. Based on the OECD-average, children whose parents did not complete secondary school have only a 15 percent chance of making it to university compared with a 60 percent chance for their peers with at least one parent who achieved tertiary-level education.

Looking at earnings across generations, 40 percent of the earnings differences between fathers carry over to the next generation. At the same time, social mobility varies a lot across countries, with a so-called "intergenerational persistence" of about 20 percent in the Nordic countries versus 70 percent or more in some of the emerging economies. This means that, thanks to the relatively low score, descendants of low income families in Scandinavia are able to achieve average pay over two to three generations. In Germany, on the other hand, where 42 percent of children with low income fathers also have a low income, it takes six generations to draw level.[110]

Who "fits in"? And does that even matter?

No matter which country and industry, more than 80 percent of employers name "fits with our culture" as one key factor for personnel selection.[111] "Obvious", one might think. After all, it is a no-brainer that companies are looking for staff that uphold their values. Who demonstrate an uncompromising service orientation if we promise "100 percent satisfaction guaranteed". That they are curious, thinking out of the box, if we are all about innovation.

Sadly though, "fit" usually has little to do with any strategic considerations or a systematic approach. It is not about company values or the ability to successfully manage business relationships and engage with important stakeholders. Instead, hiring managers tend to select candidates based on personal chemistry. "Would it be OK to get stuck with them at an airport?" is often the key hiring criterion. This question is most likely to be met by an enthusiastic "yes", if there are common interests and a similar background.

A shocking example is a survey of the biggest US law firms. Again, similar CVs were sent to potential employers. In this case, candidates had different hobbies. Education and experience were identical and always exceptional. This hardly benefitted candidates allegedly interested in soccer, country music and athletics – hobbies connected with low social status. Only in 1 percent of cases were they invited to interview. Those with an interest in classical music, sailing and polo achieved very different results, 16 percent of organizations were keen to meet them.[112]

It is not just the wrong hobby that can put an end to one's ambitions. Unspoken dress codes also help preserve social barriers. In London's financial district, "*No brown in town*" remains the rule for shoes, and a simple look at someone's feet helps to weed out "unsuitable" candidates.[113]

I know from my own experience what it means not to meet expectations. I used to work at the PR department at HP, initially as an intern supporting the press officer for printers and PCs, and afterwards one or two days per week as a student trainee. When the position of the PR manager became available I had just earned my degree. I was certain that I'd get the job. I knew the products and the media, got along well with everyone and had always delivered outstanding results. For me, the interview with the HR manager was just another meeting during a busy day at the office. Quite relaxed, I went over to her desk.

When I spoke to her, she just looked at me absent-mindedly. "I don't have time. I am waiting for an applicant", she said and returned to work. "That's me", I said happily, and got an irritated stare. In my view, the interview went just fine. Any questions regarding the way in which I'd address typical situations were a breeze. After all, I had been in that role for 1.5 years. She wasn't impressed. She considered me too young, too direct and too carefree. The t-shirt with stripes that I was wearing was the ultimate proof. It was my future boss who saved the day: "You should see the journalists", he said, and got me my first proper job.

Get yourself some help

Feedback is key to learning about unconscious reservations and biases we have. Our self-image often differs considerably from the way others see us. Their insights enable us to learn more about ourselves, thus increasing our scope of action. The "Johari window" in figure 6 helps to understand that difference in perception. The "public persona" describes what we present to others and what they perceive. It is the information about ourselves that is known to us and them, and where our perception of ourselves is aligned with that of others. This arena tends to be considerably smaller than we believe.

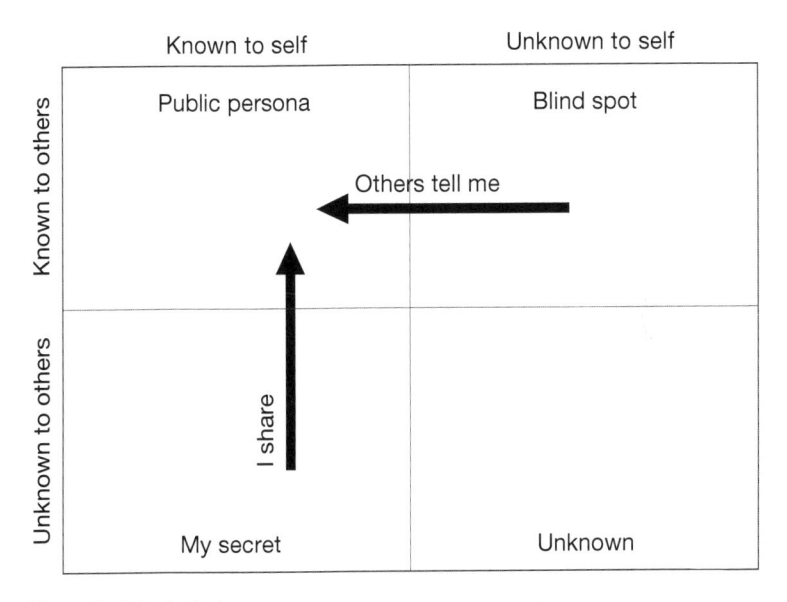

	Known to self	Unknown to self
Known to others	Public persona ← Others tell me	Blind spot
Unknown to others	My secret ↑ I share	Unknown

Figure 6: Johari window

Information that is known to me and that I don't share with others is "my secret" – for many different reasons. It could be that I don't consider that information relevant in a given context or that I don't think it matters. It could be something private or I might be embarrassed and afraid to experience social exclusion if I share it. And sometimes I believe that matters are totally obvious and there is no need to even mention them.

Often, I am wrong about that. In one experiment, participants were asked to follow one of four predefined strategies in a negotiation. Afterwards their opponents were asked which goal they had pursued. While 60 percent of negotiators were absolutely certain that they had been fully transparent, only 26 percent of their counterparts read them correctly.[114] This phenomenon is very common. Even college roommates take nine months until their perceptions become reasonably aligned.[115] Seeing that we spend not nearly as much time with most people around us, it is worthwhile to actively share information about ourselves. People who are easy to read are happier, more satisfied with their private lives and their careers and have longer and more positive relationships.[116]

Let's look at the next quadrant, the "blind spot". These are things that are unknown to myself, while others are aware of them. I can reduce my blind spot by asking for feedback. The more different the people I consult are, the more I can learn. That's because members of the outgroup will see aspects that members of my inner circle – my in-group – are also unaware of. After all, shared values, experiences and opinions mean the we are likely to interpret information in a similar way. Asking different people helps me even to gain insights into the "unknown". To learn about unconscious biases, stereotypes and belief that impact my behaviour without me – or my regular circle – being aware of them.

At the same time, differences in perspectives make it more relevant to actively share information about oneself. What I consider "normal" or "self-evident" might be perceived very differently by someone different from myself. I need to explain why I behave the way I do and the decisions I take. That helps others to understand my actions and intentions. Alternatively, it gives them a chance to point out potential errors in reasoning.

I have introduced some rules for appreciative feedback and learning conversations in Chapter 6. There is more to come in Chapter 9.

"Blind" auditioning is not just for orchestras

Where personal preferences don't matter in pre-selection and clear requirements are defined, different people are invited to interview. One technology company found that an anonymous selection process resulted in more interviewees belonging to groups underrepresented in their organization. When tasks had to be solved that are reflective of the everyday requirements that come with a role, new profiles came onto the radar: 40 percent of the candidates that made it to the second round had an educational or professional background that would have excluded them in a "regular" hiring process.[117]

Anyone hoping that artificial intelligence will revolutionize hiring any time soon, eliminating the need for targeted interventions, is most probably wrong. At the end of 2018, Amazon terminated the AI-matching project it had started with great hopes and ambitions. The issue: The system favored men for technical roles, because promising profiles were identified based on the experience of the last ten years. For roles with overwhelmingly male job holders, "female" thus became a shortcoming. But it was not just gender that created barriers. Successes that were highlighted in "historic" profiles and how they were described also affected the search criteria for promising candidates, excluding people presenting their achievements differently.[118]

LinkedIn also uses algorithms as a basis for new services. They allow organizations to match applicants with job postings. Still, "I certainly would not trust any AI system today to make a hiring decision on its own," says John Jersin, vice president of LinkedIn Talent Solutions. "The technology is just not ready yet."

This obviously does not stop people from trying. Companies like HireVue work on solutions to rate candidates in video interviews according to verbal and nonverbal cues to reduce bias in hiring. This approach does not only confront them with the familiar challenges regarding facial recognition, though – like the fact that black faces are recognized considerably less reliably than white ones. As with Amazon, results can be falsified by preferences that impacted past hires. And indeed, when tested, the outcomes reflected the previous preferences of hiring managers. Additionally, cultural differences of interviewees and how that might impact how they express themselves through gestures and the like have to be taken into account.[119]

While new solutions are heavily scrutinized for any biases inherent to the system and the potential impact of the existing database on recommendations – the familiar *"garbage in – garbage out"* – surprisingly, this is not at all the case with established solutions. Many psychometric tests help to reinforce traditional leadership behaviour.

They compare responses and preferences of current applicants with profiles that were successful in the past. This means that the candidates most likely to succeed are the ones who act today in a way that worked yesterday.

Unstructured interviews are popular and unfair

An unfair preselection is not the only barrier for anyone who does not fit our expectations of the ideal candidate. People we "like" are also advantaged in the actual interview.

While micro-aggressions – like interruptions, obviously skeptical follow-up questions or an unbelieving shake of the head – can make people we have reservations about lose their rhythm, others can be assured of our undivided and enthusiastic attention. We are happy about conclusive arguments they deliver, are interested and approachable and just about cheer them on to give their very best.

This kind of behaviour is called → *micro-affirmations* and they support our counterpart in critical phases. A friendly nod while listening, apparent agreement with what is being said or alternatively prompting them to clarify or to provide more information. We offer our own experience to strengthen the relationship or confirm our support by admitting that the situation is stressful and a question unclear or difficult.[120]

What tends to be a sign of good leadership behavior becomes an unfair advantage in this kind of situation. That is even more true as we are probably unaware of what we are doing. We won't remember that we told one candidate to just take a deep breath while persistently following up with another. That we nodded in agreement or looked irritated, shaking our head. All that remains is the impression of an engaged interesting discussion and one that just drew on like chewing gum.

Finally, unstructured interviews are the ultimate death blow to any fair selection process. Although they say little about qualification, they remain omnipresent in hiring. The problem: all those additional impressions actually distract us from relevant facts, qualifiable and quantifiable information, and dilute the basis for our decisions.[121]

Instead of a decision based on rational criteria, unstructured interviews provide optimal conditions to simply follow one's own personal preferences and gut feeling. In the end it becomes about "chemistry", which is rated more highly than the skills and experiences required to actually do the job.[122]

While many organizations collect more information than they can deal with, other companies have decided to even do away with CVs. They want to avoid being distracted by information that is not relevant for the position and fully focus on an applicant's ability to actually do the job in question.

We are not objective

There is a whole range of → *biases* that can lead us astray. Do you remember Sophie and Mandy from earlier on in this chapter? When Sophie had her first day at school, she was accompanied by both her parents. Nice people! Mother a teacher, father a chemist. Sophie was nice and well-behaved and immediately left a positive impression. This first experience impacts our perception in the longer term and also outshines experiences that might not be aligned with our initial view.

Then, there is confirmation bias: we are more likely to notice something if it is in line with our expectations. Also, we assign more relevance to these insights and remember them better. Conflicting information, on the other hand, is often not even noticed. Alternatively, we interpret it in a way that is in line with our initial assumptions (→ *Sensemaking*). If Sophie hits Mandy, we obviously don't approve of it. Still, we are pretty much persuaded that Mandy probably teased the poor child until she finally couldn't help herself any longer. After all, Mandy is always antagonizing others and she very often goes after Sophie.

Generally, people strongly overestimate their ability to make rational decisions. That's why it takes a systematic approach to ensure equal opportunities for all versus simply following our gut feeling.

One study from Texas Medical School proves this in no uncertain terms. At short notice, they were requested to increase class size by 50 students. The decision came late, the enrolment process had officially ended and all interesting candidates were already signed up. All that was left to be done was to go back to the pool of candidates that had initially been rejected and enroll 50 of the ones that had been unable to convince the selection panel in the initial round. The surprising finding? These candidates performed just as well as the ones initially selected, there was no difference apparent during either studies or at graduation. After analysis of the entry test results, researchers were able to explain this surprising finding. Students who had initially been rejected had not performed any worse in the tests based on objective criteria. Instead they had "underperformed" in unstructured interviews and it was the subjective view of the examiners that had led to them being excluded in the first round.[123]

Fair opportunities for all

To objectively assess different people, structure is required – the more, the better. Generally, the starting point should be to define the key requirements candidates need to meet. What is the position about, what are the skills someone must have in order to deliver successfully? What is the best way to assess these abilities? What possibilities exist, in order to test everyday requirements and typical challenges during the selection process? What are relevant work samples and which tasks could be assigned to support better judgements?

If "cultural fit" matters, one first needs to define what it is actually about. After all, a common interest in soccer or Japanese tea sets might make for interesting conversations, but is hardly a good indicator of whether someone will be successful in their new role. To evaluate whether someone fits culturally, a good understanding of what is core to an organization's culture is required. What is important and why? How do certain qualities and behaviors contribute to an organization's success? And how can they realistically be measured?[124] Just like with any other requirements, a structured approach is needed for tracking across candidates.

A uniform questionnaire that is consistently applied with all interviewees ensures that the same information is being captured. If some aspects are more important than others, this should be indicated up front with different numbers of points assigned to reflect their relative importance. Even if it interrupts the flow of the interview, it is important always to ask questions in the same order to ensure a fair comparison. Also, each response should be scored at once to reduce the →*halo effect*. It causes us to attribute too much weight to individual exceptionally good responses. As a result, they can outshine shortcomings that should really be taken into account.

When comparing the results of all candidates, the assessment should be done question by question rather than based on the overall impression. This increases objectivity and supports a balanced decision as opposed to being carried away by one's own excitement and an overall positive impression. At the same time, one's judgement is less susceptible to being influenced by stereotypes if several people are evaluated in parallel.[125]

Even if hiring is conducted via a panel, interviews should take place one-to-one. This prevents groupthink from impacting the flow of the discussion and the scoring. Before the alignment across the interviewers takes place, all individual scores should be consolidated. This also helps prevent that relevant information is lost due to groupthink and team dynamics.

Tips to ensure fair selection and to reflect unconscious preferences and biases

Get feedback. Ask others to help you reduce your blind spot. Don't just rely on your in-group to do that. Make a point of reaching out to people who have a very different perspective.

Avoid unstructured interviews. Take the time to consider which requirements are really important for a role. How do they show themselves in a candidate and how can they be tested? Make sure that you don't already exclude interesting profiles during pre-screening. Conduct structured interviews and make sure that groupthink does not impact decision-making.

Mentally change protagonist. Ask yourself whether you would react differently to a comment or question if it came from someone else. Someone who is younger or older, of a different gender, a different religion, ethnicity or nationality. Consider what impacts your judgement and whether there might be different ways to read a situation.

Review your inner film. Observe your reaction to the next three people you meet. What are your first thoughts? Use them as a basis to invent a short story about each person. What is their profession? What are their interests and hobbies? What are they up to? Observe the impact that age, gender, skin color, clothing, and other aspects have on your story. Give each of the people the central role in a completely different film to reduce stereotypes and biases.

Chapter 8
He doesn't look the part!

Why qualification is often not the most decisive factor for promotions

"Three candidates for the position. This is going to be an interesting discussion." Stephen looks at his HR Manager. "Do you want to introduce them?"

"Happy to. You obviously all know Peter", the colleagues smile knowingly. "Joined us straight after college. Has attended the full leadership curriculum over the years. Always demonstrated good results. Has been in his current position for about three years, so it is time for his next move."

"Do you really believe he is ready?" He's come up with some half-baked ideas lately."

"He is putting his heart and soul into the role. Sometimes overshooting the mark can be a consequence of that kind of dedication. But the position we are talking about is hardly suited for pen-pushers."

"Who else is on the list?"

"Julia. She is consistently delivering top performance. Her background is a very good fit for the position. At the same time, it would enable her to broaden her profile and to prepare for an even bigger role.

"Isn't her youngest son still small? Two years at best?"

"And this job requires a lot of travel."

"Completely agree. We shouldn't do that to either mother or child."

"I think she has that pretty much sorted out. I even believe that her husband only works part-time."

"Well, anyway. We have a responsibility here. I totally agree that Julia has a lot of potential. But we don't have to demand that of her right now."

"Who is number three?"

"Sven. For me, he has strongest profile."

"Sven!? He is a runt. What is he? 5 feet 7? Weedy. Glasses. Reedy voice. How he is ever going to pull through if things get tough?"

"And just imagine what it will look like on the outside. With customers! No one will take him seriously. He simply does not look the role."

In the last chapter I already shared a long and frustrating collection of aspects that can create barriers to people's advancement. Over the next pages, I want to make only a very few additions to that list and rather focus on the impact these aspects have on the individuals concerned. What happens with people if they feel discriminated against – and why do we regularly make such poor decisions?

Height indicator of leadership ability?

We will hear more about Julia in part 5, "Women and men". First, we will look at Sven, who is also unlikely to have been selected for the role. After all, there are at least two important aspects that shed doubts on his qualification. He is short and skinny. That is hardly aligned with a "true" leader. Study after study demonstrates: tall people are more successful.[126] Especially men. As long as they are white. The very attributes that play into their hands – tall stature, male features, decisive appearance – tend to negatively impact the opportunities of black peers, as they activate the stereotypes of the "angry black man".

For white men, though, height pays. Literally. With the same qualification and experience, tall people earn more. Two inches result in almost £1,600 annually.[127] For men, a few additional kilos can also pay off[128] – giving their opinions that extra weight. Thin men on average earn US$8,500 less than their peers. Still, overdoing it is not a good idea either. If people are believed to be lacking self-discipline, there is lower trust[129] and they are perceived as less qualified.

For women, the measure of "discipline" is way stricter. Being 25 pounds overweight results in a wage penalty of about US$14,000 compared to peers of normal weight. Being thinner is better, though. Women who are 25 pounds below average weight receive an average annual wage premium of US$15,500.

How can we ever be so mean?

That's not fair! Just like the many other reasons why we treat people differently. Anyone who wants to know why we do so, although we like to think of ourselves as decent and quite smart, needs to understand the way our brain works. Because our smart brain stands at the center of that issue.

Even in resting state, our brain requires a lot of energy. Our body invests about 20 percent of total consumption in its operation.[130] Not to mention deep thought. Anyone struggling with a complex question is left with just 50 percent of the regular body strength.[131] To make sure we don't lack the energy to hunt animals or harvest potatoes – or whatever else we do to stay alive – our brain has developed a set of brilliant and very efficient processes.

Social psychologists Susan Fiske and Shelley Taylor have developed the term "cognitive miser" for this phenomenon. If it comes to thinking, our brain behaves pretty much like Ebenezer Scrooge, only doing just as much as is absolutely required. Wherever possible, we rely on →*heuristics,* on rules of thumb – and on assumptions. Usually, that is a really smart idea. Just imagine you had to start from scratch orientating yourself on the way to the office. Didn't know where to sit at a meeting, because four legs and a back rest were insufficient indicators. If you weren't able to recognize everyday items because you could not place them.

It is only because we categorize things and simply ignore most information that we are able to cope with everyday life at all. After all, our brain receives over 11 million inputs per second and we can only consciously process 40.[132] Our perception is on auto-pilot and hardly realizes what is going on around us. Heuristics act like a spam filter. They automatically filter out many, many impressions and only let information pass that is considered relevant.[133]

That is what Nobel laureate Daniel Kahneman calls system 1 or fast thinking:[134] thinking that is rapid, automatic and unreflected. But just like with the email spam filter, sometimes information goes into trash that doesn't belong there. To avoid that, system 2 needs to take over, slow thinking.

A good way to experience the difference is the Stroop test.[135] Please name the color in which the words are printed in Figure 7. Maybe you even want to time yourself.

Black	Grey	White	White
Grey	Grey	**Black**	**Black**
White	Grey	**Black**	White
Grey	**Black**	White	White
Black	White	Grey	White

Figure 7: Stroop test

And now try the same thing with figure 8.

Black	**Grey**	**White**	White
Grey	**Grey**	Black	Black
White	Grey	Black	**White**
Grey	Black	**White**	White
Black	**White**	Grey	White

Figure 8: Stroop test

Do you recognize the difference? We can do the first list with just system 1 almost in our sleep. The shade and semantics are aligned. A really simple exercise. The second list feels different. Our brain is confronted with conflicting information. And to resolve that conflict, system 2 is required.

It is focused, reflected, weighs alternatives. That takes effort, which is why we rarely use it. While most of us are convinced that we make well considered, rational decisions, 90 percent of our thinking happens fast and intuitively, without involving system 2.

One of our most important rules of thumb is categorization. We have seen something before and something else looks similar, which makes us conclude that those two things are probably the same. From an evolution perspective that is a fabulous idea. If my buddy were eaten by a saber-toothed tiger, I had better not ask if I see a big cat approaching fast.

Behavioral patterns that once ensured our survival still impact our reactions today. An apple is an apple, a pear is a pear. If we have eaten one, it will impact our impression of others – if we ever touch them again. As a child, my mother made me try beetroot and I hated it. For 40 years I was sure that I didn't like it. One day, a friend invited me for a grand dinner. He had spent the day in the kitchen and had made beetroot risotto. There was no way I could tell him that I did not like it. And the risotto was fabulous! Since then, I eat beetroots. I still eye it with a certain skepticism, but it is a true enrichment of my menu.

In system 1, we strongly rely on pigeonholes. And we tend to make them increasingly smaller. No matter what our experience of someone is, we perceive it as typical of them. If they arrive late once, they are someone who comes late. Someone who complains once is a person looking for trouble. And we ignore minor aspects like the fact that they were stuck in an elevator or the situation was special or unfair.

Perception is reality

It is one thing for others to get a picture of me and base their decisions on it. At the same time, I have my very own idea of whether or not this is fair.

What that means is the focus of a very interesting research piece by the Center for Talent Innovation (CTI).[136] They surveyed respondents in the US to find out whether they believed they had been treated unfairly and the impact that had had. Also, they wanted to understand how personal demographics impacted their experience. Aspects like their gender, the color of their skin, whether they have a disability, their sexual orientation and identity, if they work flexibly or were born outside the US.

"Too simple", you might think. After all, you haven't necessarily been discriminated against just because you think so yourself. Maybe the fact that someone is black has nothing to do with them not being hired or promoted. But justified or not, the impression that a decision is unfair affects the person concerned. And the CTI wanted to understand how employees deal with it.

They asked employees whether their personal demographics had impacted the way they were perceived, had led to them being considered less able, less ambitious, less committed, less well-connected or whether their emotional intelligence or executive presence were put in doubt.

Feeling disadvantaged has an impact

In total, 9.2 percent of respondents in big companies said that their supervisors had treated them unfairly at times. That had an impact. Compared to those who had not experienced disadvantages they scored considerably lower. They were

- 32 percent less likely to have received a raise
- 45 percent less likely to have their job responsibilities increased
- 41 percent less likely to have received a career development opportunity
- 25 percent less likely to have received a promotion.

Those feeling disadvantaged were more likely to be angry or cynical and less proud of their company. Additionally, they invested more time in hiding part of their identity.

These negative emotions also directly impacted their employer because these employees were

- Three times as likely to plan to leave their employers within the year
- More than twice as likely to have withheld ideas or solutions in the past six months at work
- Five times as likely to speak about their company in a negative manner on social media

Anyone thinking, "Not a problem. All is well with us and it is only performance that matters", is probably wrong. Research has shown that those organizations that emphasize their merit-based culture and praise themselves for being fair often most heavily violate that very value. This is called the → *meritocracy paradox.*

Being excited about fairness can mean that people consider any activities as unfair that support individual groups of employees. There is a belief that with everyone being treated the same and evaluated based on skills and performance, there is no need for targeted interventions. Sadly, that is not the reality and companies regularly have to realize that women and minorities as well as "foreign-born" people need to work harder and show a higher performance to achieve – for example – the same income.[137]

The problem: if people are persuaded that they are truly objective, they tend not to question their decisions. They simply believe they are right and their evaluation is correct.[138] That's why the judgement of people who consider themselves extremely fair is often especially biased. Rather than just talking about equality transparency is key to identifying and addressing potential inequities.

Reducing bias in evaluations

There is a growing body of research that shows how rating systems – instead of being neutral instruments – shape the distribution of rewards in organizations. To support fair decision-making, it helps to understand the impact of personal behaviors as well as biases and to plan for them.

For example, there are considerable differences in the willingness to take risks between men and women as well as people from different cultures. This tended to have a negative impact on women on the SAT, a long-time staple of college admissions in many countries. As there was a penalty for wrong answers, they were more likely to skip questions they were uncertain about, while men tended to just guess. In the end, that was the better strategy. Statistically, the questions answered correctly by chance outweighed the penalty for wrong answers, which resulted in men in total scoring better. When no penalty was assessed for a wrong answer, all test-takers – whether men or women – answered every question.[139]

Another example: Many managers ask their team members to provide a self-assessment before their appraisal and development discussion. Again, personal demographics have a huge impact on self-evaluation. The expectations that I have about myself and the reference I use will directly influence my scoring. It depends on my self-confidence or whether I even tend to over-estimate my own abilities and performance. Whether it is OK in my culture to blow my own trumpet, or whether it is totally inacceptable. It will come as no surprise that – for similar results – people provide very different ratings.

"No problem", you might think. "I obviously take that into account." But as a result of the → *anchor effect,* the self-assessment impacts our judgement. For those rating themselves more positively then we had considered, we wonder whether we might have been too harsh. On the other hand, we start reflecting whether we might have overestimated the employees who view themselves more critically than we did. That's why it is better to abstain from asking for any up-front self-assessments.

Also, scale can impact how different people are being evaluated, with a shorter one providing a more balanced rating. In one experiment, students were presented with an identical lecture transcript and were asked to score it on a 10- or 6-point-scale respectively. The alleged gender of the instructor was assigned randomly. The scale used significantly affected the size of the gender gap in evaluations in the most male-dominated fields. For the students, a 10 represented an outstanding performance, true brilliance, which was much more likely to be assigned to men. While great lectures of "John" were awarded a 10, "Julie" rather scored an 8 or a 9. With a 6-point-scale, that bias disappeared. It only required a very good performance to be awarded the top rating. While "John" still tended to be judged more positively, "Julie's" performance was considered sufficient to justify a 6.[140] This makes it a typical example of how → *Framing* – the way in which we present information as well as the context we provide – can support a fair judgement.

Systematically address typical mental short cuts

It is most important, though, not to simply rely on instinct. We need to question our gut feeling and examine whether stereotypes, preferences or (unconscious) biases impact our perception and behavior. There are more than 200 such biases at play in different situations that can impact our judgement. Accordingly, it is totally impossible to keep track of them all. This is why Buster Benson's "Cognitive Bias Cheat Sheet" is such a helpful tool (see figure 9).[141]

COGNITIVE BIAS CHEAT SHEET
BECAUSE THINKING IS HARD

1 TOO MUCH INFO
SO ONLY NOTICE...
- CHANGES
- BIZARRENESS
- REPETITION
- CONFIRMATION

2 NOT ENOUGH MEANING
SO FILL IN GAPS WITH...
- PATTERNS
- GENERALITIES
- BENEFIT OF DOUBT
- EASIER PROBLEMS
- OUR CURRENT MINDSET

3 NOT ENOUGH TIME
SO ASSUME...
- WE'RE RIGHT
- WE CAN DO THIS
- NEAREST THING IS BEST
- FINISH WHAT'S STARTED
- KEEP OPTIONS OPEN

4 NOT ENOUGH MEMORY
SO SAVE SPACE BY...
- EDITING MEMORIES DOWN
- GENERALIZING
- KEEPING AN EXAMPLE
- USING EXTERNAL MEMORY

Figure 9: Cognitive Bias Cheat Sheet

This overview clusters the many, many different factors that can result in unfair decisions according to four different causes. Being aware of these factors is helpful to reflect upon one's own behavior and make better decisions.

We have too much information

We only notice what is different, unusual, repetitive or confirms our existing believes.

Rather than getting overwhelmed by way too much information, consider what is truly relevant. What is most important for a job or a project? What qualifies someone to take it on? Are there any elements that could help stretch a team member to learn something new or develop additional skills? Then focus on what matters most.

What we know doesn't make sense

If there is information missing, we fill that blanks ourselves. We generalize, fall for stereotypes and rely on our own interpretation.

Before taking any important decision, check what you really know against what you believe. Do you really have the information required to achieve a good outcome? What could be missing and how can you get a hold of that data?

We don't have enough time

You really want to call it a day. Have to leave on time. Just quickly finish this action and be off as soon as you can.

If we are stressed or tired, the conditions are perfect for stereotypes and assumption to guide our decisions. That's why it is a good idea to postpone important ones to the next day and get back to them with a fresh mind. Additionally, our circadian rhythm – whether we are an early bird or a night owl – impacts the decision quality. Consider your personal preferences and also make sure to take breaks. Your head deserves them.

We don't have enough capacity

Sometimes, providing feedback is more difficult than expected. Suddenly we can't remember any examples we meant to provide. Or a discussion gets out of hand and in the end no one even remembers what it was really about.

In such cases, it is good to have notes or put flipcharts with key questions up on the walls. Helping our head to focus makes sure that we are less likely to overlook what truly matters. Maybe you have had that experience yourself when taking a walk: if we need to concentrate hard, for example to provide an argument, we often stop walking. That is a typical attempt of our body to economize – there is more energy left for thinking.

Considering what happened until now

Remembering in a given situation that our brain likes to take short cuts and finding ways to make sure that does not have a negative impact on decisions is one thing. Also, as a leader, you should take some time to reflect on what has happened before. Just like with the recaps of your favorite TV show. Because most situations have a history, a series of events and experiences that have impacted our perception. There are many incidents, for example, that lead up to the decision to give someone a bigger role, a salary increase or a promotion. Many of those were discussed over the last chapters. Who takes on what responsibilities? Who is being asked? Who is being listened to?

To check whether one is doing justice to all team members, another analysis is helpful. This one involves mapping one's team on a "competence and trust matrix" (see figure 10).

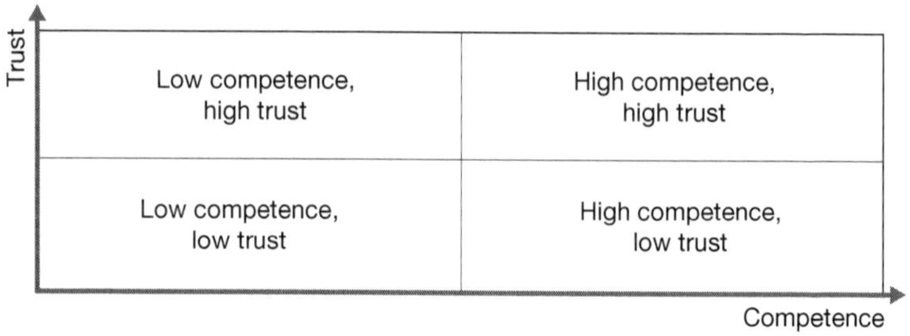

Trust	Low competence, high trust	High competence, high trust
	Low competence, low trust	High competence, low trust

Competence

Figure 10: The competence and trust matrix provides a new perspective on one's team

Who do you consider especially competent? Who continuously delivers great performance? Who takes on complex or critical tasks and always delivers? Who do you trust? Who you rely on if the going gets tough? Who do you include earlier than others or more often in critical or confidential projects?

Having mapped your team based on these criteria, the next step is to understand your reasoning. Who is placed where? Why? What are the aspects that impact your perception? What is the reason you considered someone extremely or less competent? What is the basis for that judgement? Why do you consider some team members more trustworthy than others? Did the ones you trust less give you any reason for that perception? Did they let you down? Or is it simply that you feel more at ease and comfortable with others?

What is the impact of individual placements? How do they impact your behavior? Who gets more appreciation, who gets less? Who has better or worse opportunities to shine? Who gets visibility – also beyond one's own department, and has the opportunity to build relevant contacts?

As has been demonstrated again and again, there are many aspects that impact the perception of someone's competence, which have nothing whatsoever to do with their abilities. Also, their actual reliability has little influence on the trust placed in a person. Way more important are commonalities, similar values or experiences.

Anyone honestly conducting this analysis probably has some eye-opening moments and is likely to realize that they don't do justice to all members of their team. That not everyone is being treated fairly. Being aware and understanding what is actually going on, and the consequences of this, is a defining moment. It creates the basis for a concrete plan and enables leaders to take action in order to overcome inequity.

Tips to do justice to different people

Become aware of your own stereotypes. What do you think are typical traits of women, the elderly, people of a different social class or members of another group? What is the basis for your judgement? How would you feel if someone else drew conclusions about you and your behavior based on similar insights?

Find common ground. Discuss what you have in common instead of focusing on the things that differentiate you. Finding things in common does not only create an atmosphere of trust and safety. It also primes someone to see the other as a member of their in-group – with all the advantages that come with that status.

Rely on your own judgement versus that of others. If acquaintances and people we trust tell us something negative about someone else, this has an impact on our perception. Instead of approaching that person with an open mind, we tend to be on the lookout for information that confirms their judgement. That is because of confirmation bias.

Be curious. Ask others how they experience their environment, while trying to avoid three pitfalls: judging them, stereotypes or asking for information that is just none of your business. Ask for support if needed. Tell them you know too little about a topic but are eager to learn, that you have a serious interest but are afraid of making mistakes. Show that you are vulnerable instead of trying to look strong.

Chapter 9
I didn't yet have a chance to provide feedback

Why we sometimes avoid giving feedback and how to make it work

"John has been putting in a much weaker performance." Peter frowns, looking at his noodles with irritation. "In the past, he regularly came up with new, out-of-the box ideas and challenged us with unconventional ideas. Lately, … not so much."

"Do you know why?"

"No idea. I think he doesn't get along well with Yasmin. His reaction to her is always extremely critical. He seems to struggle with the fact that others have good ideas, too. I somehow get the impression that he is looking for something different."

"Did you talk to him?"

"Not yet. There was no opportunity. Currently, I am super busy and quite stressed. That's why I have no intention to open a whole new can of worms."

"Still, would be good if you talked to him."

"Sure, I will. Just not now. And you know: you shouldn't hold up travelers."

"That's certainly true. By the way, did you respond to the HR request, yet. Nominate someone for the upcoming leader program?"

"Not yet. I still want to think about it."

"Maybe John is an option?"

"Hardly. The way things are playing out at the moment, it is really not the right time."

Anyone wanting to avoid addressing disagreements and conflict at work is in good company. About 30 percent of employees prefer to avoid confrontations at work. In comparison: not even 20 percent mind ending a relationship.[142]

Apparently, people are good at not following up if they feel discomfort. According to a survey, just 36 percent of supervisors finish performance evaluations fully and on time. About two in three of HR executives said that their biggest performance management challenge is managers' inability or unwillingness to have difficult feedback discussions. Employees are dissatisfied, too. More than half say their most recent performance review was unfair or inaccurate, and one in four dreads such evaluations more than anything else in their working lives.[143]

Those that are "different" tend to not just get less feedback, it is also less concrete and helpful and gets postponed more often. There are multiple reasons for that behaviour. Managers can find it more difficult to give and are afraid that they might be blamed for discrimination. That makes them hesitate. Also, they feel less connected with people different from themselves, which makes it less worth their effort.[144] Especially employees who work internationally – outside their home country – often struggle with the feedback they get. Because it is vague, unclear or ambiguous. Because they are judged against rules they don't know or understand. Or because it builds on standards that are not well aligned with their culture or value system.[145]

The situation also is unsatisfactory for women. They not only get less development-oriented feedback than their male peers.[146] Also, it tends to be less specific, less constructive and helpful. Managers say that the reason for this is fear of hurting their feelings or making them cry. But once they get started, they tend to really dish out: women get considerably more negative and hurtful feedback.

He is decisive, she is aggressive

An analysis of annual performance reviews showed that women receive more subjective feedback and that it is often tainted by gender stereotypes. Either different expectations impact the judgement – meaning that people are measured against unequal standards – or the same behavior is interpreted differently. That happens, for example, if women are perceived as indecisive, when men are seen as carefully weighing different options. She could be said to "seem paralyzed and confused when facing tight deadlines to make decisions," while "he seems hesitant in making decisions, yet he is able to work out multiple alternative solutions and determined to find the most suitable one." Such double standards clearly affect women's opportunities for advancement.[147]

There is a second problem: While critical feedback that men get is almost always constructive and provides practical tips about how to improve, women are often confronted with negative reactions that are personal and don't include helpful advice. While he is being told "Hone your strategies for guiding your team and developing their skills. It is important to set proper guidance around priorities and to help as needed in designs and product decisions", she hears "You can come across as abrasive sometimes. I know you don't mean to, but you need to pay attention to your tone", or "Your peers sometimes feel that you don't leave them enough room. Sometimes you need to step back to let others shine."[148]

Whether they are praised or criticized, the feedback women get tends to be less meaningful for their development. Men are provided with a full picture of what they did well, why it was good and what to do to improve further. Additionally, they get advice on where else to focus to give them extra visibility and an opportunity to increase responsibilities. Women are just told "that was great" or "well done". While that might sound good initially, performance management systems tell a different story. For women – unlike men – vague feedback correlates with lower performance ratings. If they don't get proper feedback, women have fewer opportunities to improve, and it creates barriers to their career. [149]

Feeling safe impacts the support we give

Obviously, it is not just gender that affects the likelihood of receiving feedback, as well as what an employee gets to hear. Chapter 3 dealt with homophily, the fact that we predominantly know people similar to ourselves. In their presence we feel comfortable. It is easier to address an issue, because we have a better idea of how they might react and are less afraid of making an embarrassing mistake. Also, they are unlikely to cry. Discussions across demographic differences, on the other hand – like gender, age, personal or cultural background – often feel considerably more difficult, which is why we are more prone to postpone them. Also, there simply are fewer – especially informal – opportunities to address an issue before it has developed into something massive.

To create fair conditions, though, it is not only important to meet more different people. It is also insufficient only to recognize how one's own experiences and values impact perspective and judgement. It is just as important to find appropriate ways to offer and provide appreciative feedback that works across differences.

To understand why our tips and recommendations can easily be ever so slightly off target, it is helpful to understand the four phases of learning and how they can create a deceptive feeling of security or unjustified panic (see figure 11).

Generally, we start each new situation unconsciously incompetent. We have no clue what there is to know and therefore have no benchmark to measure ourselves against. We are in a phase of blissful ignorance and tend to completely over-estimate ourselves. This is called the → *Dunning-Kruger effect*.

After we have bloodied our noses a few times, we recognize that we have underestimated the complexity of an issue and that it would be worthwhile to dig a bit deeper. We start engaging with a topic, to research, read and learn. During this phase we are consciously incompetent and tend to feel inadequate and totally overwhelmed by the subject.

	Competence	
Consciousness	Concsious incompetence →	Conscious competence ↓
	↑ Unconscious incompetence	Unconscious competence

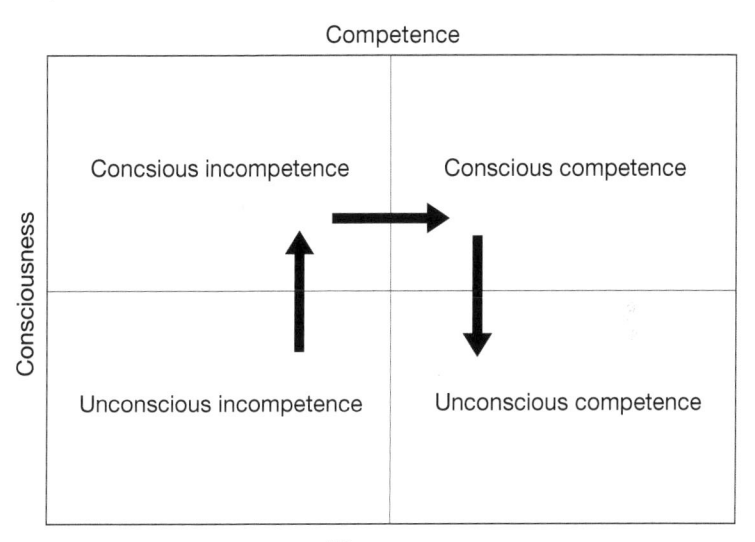

Figure 11: Four phases of learning[150]

Over time, we manage to develop more knowledge and a better understanding and get better at mastering new situations. Initially, that requires our full attention and a lot of energy. We need to prepare for every discussion, each intervention, to successfully overcome the challenges involved.

The more we practice, the easier it becomes to act appropriately, and finally we feel we can manage in our sleep. Our new knowledge has become part of our flesh and blood and we have reached the phase of unconscious competence. It has finally become like riding a bike. It works automatically without having to remind ourselves to pedal.

How that is related to feedback? The model emphasizes that we are blind to many things that others perceive. With growing competence, we become more aware of that fact and can react more appropriately.

Also, the model provides hope. Even if it is initially hard to provide good and meaningful feedback, it gets easier with time.

Providing safety

How is my appeal to consider the individual situation aligned with the growing call for full transparency? With a completely open feedback culture like the one Netflix is praised for? There is no question at all that immediate and honest feedback are important for personal development. But if you don't just want to share your opinion but truly want to help others grow, a couple of aspects must be considered.

On the one hand, feedback can create fear. People who are already uncertain about their performance need encouragement and support, instead of destroying them for good. Because it is not about learning in the panic zone but sheer survival.

If we believe that we can develop and improve, on the other hand, we make extra efforts. We work harder and enjoy the progress we make. Rather than being paralyzed by the fear of doing anything wrong, we accept mistakes as part of learning and test our boundaries. At the same time, we enjoy our work more thoroughly and our motivation increases. As a result, we make fewer mistakes.[151]

Psychological safety is essential to be able to take feedback on board. One way to provide it is proper framing. How we act and what we say is an indicator for others, whether there is reason for concern or panic or whether we have their best interests at heart. If someone tells us with a red face to come to their office immediately, we'll feel very different about that compared to being asked to join someone for some feedback over a cup of coffee.

According to Daniel Coyle, author of *The Culture Code*, one way to provide feedback has proven to be especially effective: "I am giving you these comments because I have very high expectations and I know that you can reach them." Students who were approached in this way revised their papers far more often than peers, and their performance improved significantly.

What is special: people addressed this way get three important cues that show them their efforts are worthwhile:[152]

- You are part of this group.
- This group is special; we have high standards here.
- I believe you can reach these standards.

That not only conveys belonging and appreciation. It also triggers a learning mindset, one that makes us open for new challenges.

Providing feedback that helps growth

It is just as important to highlight things that go well. Distinguishing oneself and being successful work best based on someone's strengths. This requires not just focusing on mistakes but doing more of the things that a person is good at and that set them apart. Especially if people are different, their strategies for success will also differ. That's why feedback is not about helping someone else to be just like oneself but to support them in becoming the best possible version of themselves.

The most effective strategy is to immediately point out things they do well and that impress us. Saying that something works for us and why. That we would like to see more of it and why we believe it is worthwhile. These are the moments when members of your team experience what "good" looks like and how it feels. It becomes a concrete experience. They can reflect upon what they have done, which other situations would call for the same behavior, and they gain a new and effective tool for their work.[153]

When criticizing what worked less well, on the other hand, it is not about what "went wrong" or "must be changed". After all, I can only speak for myself, what it did (or didn't do) for me, the impact it had. Alternatively, I can say how I would have behaved in similar circumstances, thus raising awareness for possible alternative approaches. After all, I am not the measure of all things. My impressions are mine. They are based on a matching what I have experienced with my own ideas and expectations – not an ultimate truth. That also affects the feedback we should give (see table 9).

Instead of	Try
Can I give you some feedback?	Here's my reaction.
Good job!	Here are three things that really worked for me. What was going through your mind when you did them?
Here's what you should do.	Here's what I would do.
Here's where you need to improve.	Here's what worked best for me, and here's why.
That didn't really work.	When you did x, I felt y or I didn't get that.
You need to improve your communication skills.	Here's exactly where you started to lose me.
You need to be more responsive.	When I don't hear from you, I worry that we're not on the same page.
You lack strategic thinking.	I'm struggling to understand your plan.
You should do x [in response to a request for advice].	What do you feel you're struggling with, and what have you done in the past that's worked in a similar situation?

Table 9: Help team members to shine (Marcus Buckingham and Ashley Goodall)

Even if someone actively seeks your advice, you shouldn't immediately share your tips. It is more helpful in that situation to first ask what is currently working well. Doing so shifts focus from a place of concern and a perceived failure to a feeling of self-efficacy. There are things I am good at and manage well. People no longer sit like a rabbit looking at a snake. It even alters their brain chemistry so that they are open to new solutions and different ways of thinking or acting.

The next step is thinking about the past: when did something like this happen before? What worked then? This creates the basis for tackling the future: What do you already know? What should you do? In your experience, what has worked in a similar situation? On this basis, you can then of course share your own experience.[154]

The advantage: rather than bothering with the "why" or trying to copy someone else's approach, the focus is on practical solutions that promise to be successful in this very situation.

Another strategy helps the brain to orient itself: avoid sandwich feedback. Although it is often recommended as a great solution to package negative feedback and making it easier to swallow, it creates confusion in our minds. Our brain simply does not know what to do with all that conflicting information and does what it is best at: it picks and chooses and goes with the messages that resonate the most. Anyone insecure and self-critical only gets the negative. People brimming with self-esteem, on the other hand, leave that discussion happily believing that their boss is just as pleased and can hardly hold back.

But whether positive or development-oriented, feedback should always be connected with performance or goals. Not just saying that someone did not actively contribute to a meeting, but also mentioning that this means the team misses out on an important perspective, will be able to achieve more.

Building trust

As familiarity helps to address difficult topics, I want to introduce a model developed by Edgar and Peter Schein focused on transformational leadership.

In contrast to the so-called transactional leadership (level 1), which means that managers tell their staff what to do and they simply follow those directions, transformational leadership (level 2) builds on cooperative, trusting relationships that are not just focused on the matter at hand.

In a complex work environment marked by intensive competition, radical technological change and a continuously changing ecosystem, level 1 leadership has lost its usefulness for almost all disciplines. In any environment that relies on sharing and developing ideas in cooperation, on building on each other to solve problems and achieve results, cooperative leadership is called for. And trust is a key enabler in that context.

In Chapter 8, you have already analyzed whether and how the relationships with individual members of your team differ. The competence and trust matrix provides a great starting point to develop a relationship map, as introduced by Peter and Edgar Schein in their book *Humble Leadership*.[155]

This map enables you to visualize your connections with key stakeholders – those people who have expectations towards you – and you can indicate the strength of your relationships. "L1" (Level 1) stands for transactional, which means working together based on common rules and according to professional standards. L2 relationships are characterized by cooperation, readiness to help and trustful collaboration. L3 are emotionally intimate relationships with mutual commitments. By the size and positioning of the bubbles, the distance as well as the strength of the arrows, you can visualize the relevance and quality of different relationships.

For Peter, the picture would probably look something like figure 12:

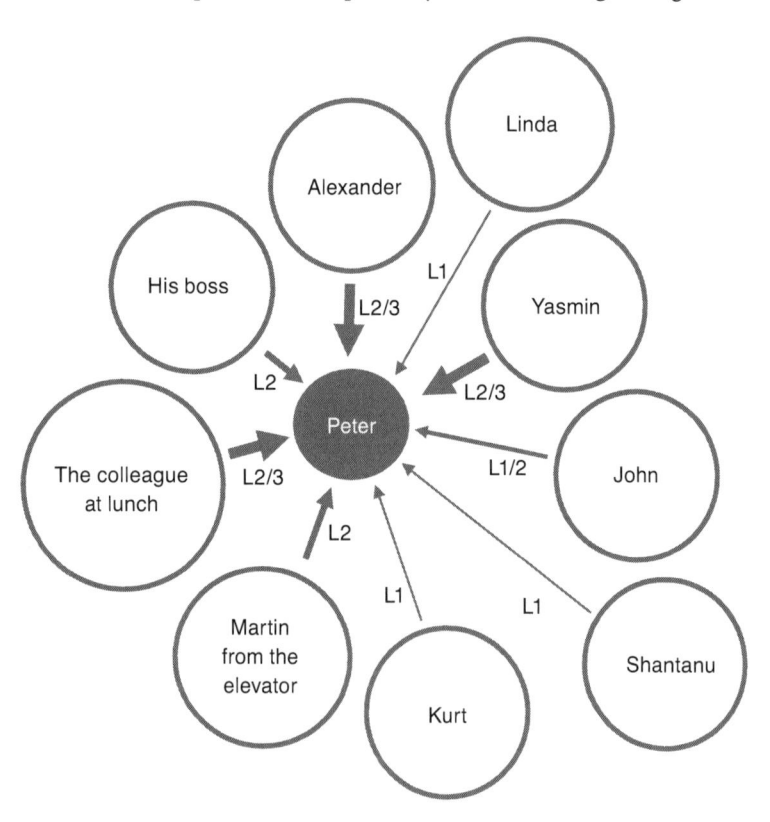

Figure 12: Relationship map according to Edgar H. and Peter A. Schein

134 Fair Leadership

As one can easily see, he does not feel equally close to different members of his team. There isn't the same level of connectedness either. Maybe that is OK for him. Still, anyone wanting to improve the quality of individual relationships needs to be proactive. Just like with feedback, it helps to focus on what works, on positive experiences from the past. And this is how it is done:

- **Find out what works.** Concentrate on your level 2 connections first. Note what happened that resulted in a deeper connection. What did you do? What did others do? What enabled you to build rapport? What was the reason that you started recognizing team members as people versus just somebody filling a role? What behaviors and opportunities led to you trusting some over others and developing a personal relationship?
- **Look for patterns.** Find the commonalities regarding behaviors or situations.
- **Replicate success.** Consider how to apply the same mechanisms to other relationships.

That's where it helps to go back to the notes you made regarding the competence and trust matrix from Chapter 8. This is where you have already pondered factors that impact your relationships – with possible reservations, the impact of stereotypes, with past experiences that have affected your view.

Now it is time to explore how the things that you know about individual members of your team differ, depending on how familiar you are with them. Which are the pieces of information that matter most? What information would help you to also build a stronger link with others? Consider whether it is OK to ask them. If so, think about the best possible way to go about it.

That means creating a concrete plan. Just thinking "it would be quite nice to get to know Julia better" or "I'll get to that eventually" will most probably be insufficient. Instead it means clearly formulating goals: "I want to identify three things that I have in common with Julia in order to strengthen our relationship." That is the basis to decide what is needed and to create an action plan.

To follow through, it helps to consider the advantages. What it feels like. Why it matters. Why it is worthwhile. And afterwards, to also consider barriers. Everything that could keep you from achieving your goals. Maybe you are embarrassed because you know hardly anything about some members of your team? Maybe you are concerned that Julia might complain because she feels ill-treated? Dealing with both, advantages and barriers is called mental contrasting, and it is an extremely successful approach to setting goals and following through afterwards.[156]

Tips for feedback and to strengthen relationships

Convey that it is worth the effort. Connect development-oriented feedback with the following three messages: You belong to us. We have very high standards. You can meet them. Give concrete feedback that people can build on.

Consider the signals you might convey unconsciously. Think about the impact that your appearance or your tone of voice might have on the situation. Do you use such aspects consciously? Do they support your message or could they distort it?

Tell people what they do well. Best to do it immediately. Help others to learn from their strengths. That works best if they get immediate feedback about things done well. Be concrete. Tell them what you liked, why, and the impact it had on you.

Help people to develop their own solutions. Rather than providing tips that have worked for you, it is often more helpful to support team members in finding solutions based on their experience. Start focusing on the positive: What works well currently? Only afterwards look at the issue at hand. Ask when they experienced something similar. What helped in that situation? What are the elements they can transfer to the challenge they are currently facing?

Strengthen ties. Develop a relationship map to identify where to take action. To strengthen relationships, leverage strategies that have proven successful in other situations.

PART 4
REMOTE, DIGITAL AND INTERNATIONAL

Nowadays, fewer and fewer teams still sit together all in the same place. That creates new challenges in collaboration, especially when cultural difference also come into play.

A flexible workplace is often praised as the ultimate key to a better work-life-balance. But it can get lonely for staff and even become a barrier to their career. People who are part of a matrix or an international team, who generally work based away from their teams, are faced with similar issues. Why this is so and what can be done to overcome barriers is what Chapter 10, "*Out of sight, out of mind*", is about.

You might sometimes think "*That sounds Greek to me*" when collaborating internationally. Reason enough to read Chapter 11 and gain insights into the way that cultural differences impact collaboration.

Today, being part of international projects is a reality for many employees. At the same time, different values and norms provides a lot of opportunity for conflict. Before complaining "That's never going to work!", it is worth taking a look at Chapter 12.

Chapter 10
Out of sight, out of mind

Why distance impacts opportunities and how to address that

Coffee in hand Alexander rolls up to Curt's desk with his chair. "I have a question about the board presentation."

"Hm?"

"I am done with the first version. Still, some of the messages are not as clear as I'd like. Could you take a look?"

"Sure. Happy to. Did you ask Linda, though? She used to work in strategy. She has done tons."

"I know. But she's not around. Home office. I want to get this done now. Might ask her later if the opportunity arises."

In the 1970s, MIT professor Thomas J. Allen made a surprising discovery. On behalf of the US government he was looking into factors that affect the success of complex technical projects. One pattern was immediately apparent: the most successful projects where driven by sets of individuals who formed "clusters of high communicators". He dug into the data to better understand what they had in common and came across an unexpected commonality.

Being "close" to someone tends to be true – literally

The decisive factor was the distance between their desks. It stood in direct correlation to how often they talked. "We could see, just through the frequency, without knowing where they sat, who was on each floor", says Allen. "Something as simple as visual contact is very, very important, more important than you might think. If you can see the other person or even the area where they work, you're reminded of them, and that brings a whole bunch of effects."[157]

Frequency of communication

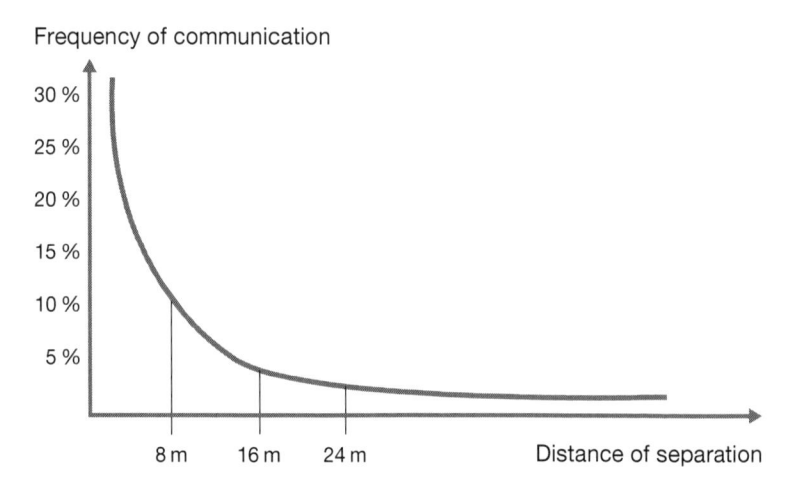

Figure 13: The Allen-Curve shows the connection between physical distance and frequency of interactions

Since then the world has changed. Social media, video services and a growing number of tools supporting collaboration shrink distances. Cooperating across sites should have ceased to be a challenge. The Allen curve (figure 13), depicting the correlation between distance and frequency of interactions, should be a thing of the past. But Allen made a different discovery: "Rather than finding that the probability of telephone communication increases with distance, as face-to-face probability decays, our data show a decay in the use of all communication media with distance."[158]

A huge relocation project gave an e-commerce firm the opportunity to understand the impact of changing seating arrangements in real life. Based on the analysis of almost 40 000 deals, they found that staff sitting in a new environment made 40 percent more revenue on average. This was despite the fact that they did not collaborate directly with the colleagues around them. Just to overhear discussions and informal dialog was sufficient to spark ideas and offer new solutions to customers rather than simply relying on what worked in the past[159].

Proximity does not just impact creativity. It also accelerates careers. With the same performance level, people working from home are faced with an up to 50 percent slower progression.[160] One of the reasons is that they have 25 percent fewer development conversations, a factor that especially impacts employees at earlier career stages.[161] Also, they are given lower job evaluations and are proposed for lower pay increases.[162]

You pay for distance, but proximity does not come cheap either

"Message received, everyone back to the office", you might think. But it is not quite that simple – a lesson that Marissa Meyer had to learn the hard way at Yahoo.

In view of the growing support for Fridays for Future, let's start by looking at the ecological advantages of working from home. Surprisingly, just two percent of respondents recently named "Sustainability/Eco-responsibility/Reduce Carbon Footprint" as having a strong influence on their decision to implement alternative workplace programs. In 2011, it was one in four.[163] The impact is massive, though. If those with compatible jobs and a desire to work from home did so just half the time, the greenhouse gas reduction would be the equivalent of taking the entire New York State workforce permanently off the road. The national savings would total over $700 billion a year. A typical business would save $11,000 per person annually, the remote workers between $2,000 and $7,000. The Congressional Budget Office estimates the entire five-year cost of implementing remote working throughout government at $30 million. This is compared to $100 million in lost productivity from a single-day shutdown of federal offices in Washington DC due to snow.[164]

At the same time, employees working from home are more productive. In one frequently cited study, researchers found a 13 percent increase in performance as they made fewer breaks, had fewer sick days and were interrupted less frequently. At the same time, job satisfaction increased and there was lower turnover.[165]

Additionally, remote working is a trend that can hardly be stopped. Today, 43 percent of employees work away from their teams at least part of time and even more want to do so. And it is not just employee expectations and an increasing request for flexibility that drives more dispersed teams. At least as important are changing business requirements. Many firms have ambitious real estate plans with sizable office space reductions. Also contributing is the growing importance of agile teams and flash organizations, as well as collaboration across a matrix, which has become a reality for 84 percent of employees in some way or form.[166]

And another trend is key: market changes. New growth markets and geographies that host innovation centers or are being used as extended workbenches. They simply are somewhere else and that is not going to change. Nonetheless, distance does impact careers and decreases the probability that it is truly the best-qualified people who are assigned to key projects. Often, they are not even aware of exiting career opportunities. These might be assigned informally. Or potential candidates don't know the right people or are not at the right place at the right time.

That's why companies – instead of trying to turn back time – are well advised to find solutions that enable employees to engage fully and succeed no matter where they work.

In remote teams, belonging doesn't simply happen

Creating the same kind of connectedness across distance that comes more easily with in-person interactions requires an active approach.

Also, to build strong relationships, it is not enough to focus on business transactions only. Social aspects of collaboration need to be translated into the virtual environment as well.

Not all leaders are up for that challenge, yet: Employees based apart from their teams are more likely to feel disconnected from their manager according to a recent survey.[167] This does not only impact the one-to-one relationship. These respondents are almost six times more likely to also feel disconnected from their peers and more than five times as likely to say that they lack access to information that is needed to do a good job. Also, and not surprisingly, they are considerably more likely to say they would leave given an interesting opportunity.

To strengthen belonging, three aspects must be considered: supporting technology, common rules and established practices.

By now, there are many interesting tools and platforms to support collaboration. To find those that best meet the needs of your team, different degrees of affinity with technology need to be considered. Also, it is worth remembering, that IT support – which tends to be limited in many of today's offices – is probably non-existent at home. A fabulous solution that creates insurmountable barriers for half of your team is not going to yield any improvements. In that case, it is better to go with a simple approach and add functionality as everyone gains confidence using it. Lowering standards is just as important, if technological requirements are not met at all sites. In that case it is more inclusive to go for a minimum common approach and put everyone on equal footing.

Technology is not an aim in itself. Instead it needs to support the goal of different interactions. If it is about getting to know each other, you will achieve faster progress if participants do not just hear but also see each other. If you want to discuss documents, everyone should be able to see what is being discussed. In order to create true connections, though, a common platform is not enough. As in real life, it requires identifying appropriate activities that help build trust. If at all possible, this should include meeting face-to-face and not just virtually.

Day-to-day interactions

Those of us based in an office with our team underestimate, just how much information is transmitted by just being in the situation without saying a word. Seeing what the desk looks like. Whether a colleague simply looks at you with blank eyes in response to your invitation for coffee or if she does not even raise her head. All these are clear indicators whether you can dump another project on them just now. Whether it is OK if we are late with our contribution or if it might be a good idea to offer support. All of these hints are invisible to anyone working remotely.

That's why clear communications and common agreements are critical, as are rules that everyone adheres to as well as a certain discipline regarding contacts and the exchange of information. What might appear overly formal is actually an indispensable aid in a decentralized team – even more so if it also spans different national cultures.

For meetings, for example, that means to always prepare an agenda that includes starting and end times – as well as breaks if the session is long. Consider the needs of different locations in the way you work to avoid frustration on the part of team members based remotely. The use of mobile video equipment for conference rooms helps ensure they have a more similar work experience. Staff dialing in can see who is speaking and what is going on. If solutions like this are unavailable, consider other mechanisms that enable them to participate more fully.

- Ask employees dialing in to facilitate the discussion to avoid disengaging them in the heat of the moment.
- Agreeing that everyone dials in if just one person has to make sure that all the team is on equal footing.
- For each topic discussed, go around your virtual table to ensure everyone can share their input.
- Whether in or outside the room, keep a tally list of who spoke how many times to help balance the discussion.
- If there has been a long silence on the line, check in to understand what the matter might be.

Seemingly trivial, but often overlooked: consider time zones in your planning and rotate meeting times if applicable. In a recent poll, participants from Europe and the US largely agreed that time difference has no serious impact on their work. The view from East Asia was markedly different, with two in three respondents saying that it had a strong or massive impact. They tended all too often to find themselves participating in calls that took place in the dead of night or at the crack of dawn.[168]

In the end, it is about making sure that those behaviors that support working across locations become second nature. That they are the standard way of working for a team rather than grudgingly practiced exceptions that require special attention. Remember the four stages of learning from chapter 9? Unconscious competence, that's what we are aiming for.

To achieve this level of "normal", it is not enough to concentrate on business transactions across the team. If some team members work remotely regularly or even always, it becomes important to translate social aspects of collaboration into the virtual environment. That can be supported by virtual coffee chats or social media groups that allow team members to get a glimpse of each other's daily lives or follow them to conferences and events.

It also helps to use status updates to let everyone know whether you are available and can be disturbed. Agreeing on common core hours can also be useful, to help colleagues plan for a good time to reach out. At least as important are solutions that allow for asynchronous collaboration, enabling team members to contribute in their own time while making sure that ideas and perspectives don't get lost.

Create "tie" as a leader

Lower levels of support, lower performance ratings, lower pay. At the beginning of this chapter, I made the point that team members who are less visible also tend to be less appreciated by their managers. Maybe you have found the same to hold true when analyzing the competence & trust matrix in Chapter 8? That physical proximity increases trust in your team? That you know more about the work of those around you and that you consider them more competent? Maybe the relationship map from Chapter 9 indicates that physical distance also shows on paper?

It might be worthwhile to return to those exercises and to check whether distance has an impact and how contacts might differ. Whether employees working at other sites are similarly likely to be part of discussions and involved at the same stage as those at the very next desk. Whether you tend to share thoughts over a cup of coffee – just not virtually. In case you recognize an imbalance, find ways to straighten it. Engage actively with remote team members to bring them on board. Reach out regularly. Plan for meetings and simply give them a call. Create checklists to ensure that people who are not in the office still remain visible to you (more about checklists in Chapter 14).

Another way to ensure action is "if-then" planning. It addresses the issue that "I'll get to that eventually" very often does not happen. Good intentions are simply not enough. Instead, saying "if it is Tuesday, then I'll give Linda a call" is way more likely to yield results. Planning like that has a 300 percent higher probability of successful outcomes. "If-then" is a language that our mind understands exceptionally well. We remember such plans better and they guide behavior even unconsciously because our subconscious mind scans the environment for the "if"-situation. This enables you to seize the moment even when you are busy doing other things. Because you have formulated what to do up front, it is also extremely simple to act upon your intentions when the time arises.[169]

Everyone who has concerns this could still be insufficient, can go one step further. In that case you also plan for alternative scenarios. For the unlikely event of anything preventing you from that call. For example, "If I am traveling on Tuesday, I will ask a colleague to get in touch with Linda." This even supports stronger connections across the whole team.

Tipps for overcoming distance

Be a role model. Regularly work remotely yourself and talk about it. This not only demonstrates to others that it is OK for them, too, it also helps you to understand and consequently address barriers.

Make people visible who are not physically present in the office. Use your camera for calls and profile pictures for apps. Put a picture or photo montage of your full team up on the wall, your desk or your desktop.

Stay in touch. Regularly call team members working remotely. Have a short chat with no set agenda. Have a coffee together and discuss what's on your mind. If you recognize you don't follow through, plan 15-minute slots several times during your week for a virtual walk around and get in touch with all your team.

Integrate members in the full team. Successful teams are completely interconnected. Use tools and solutions to get everyone in touch, for example through short unstructured calls that establish new connections and help communalities and different perspectives to surface.

Chapter 11
That sounds Greek to me

Why it is normal that others behave differently even if it puzzles me

"I had pictured that differently." Peter uses the time over lunch to complain about his new Indian team member who does not live up to expectations at all. "He went to a top school and came with great references."

"What's the problem?"

"I was keen to get someone on my team who provides a very different perspective. Who questions things. But Shantanu just sits in our meetings with a friendly smile on his face."

"Did you talk to him and ask?"

"Sure! With any discussion. I regularly reach out and say: 'So. Shantanu, what do you think?' But he just says something noncommittal."

"Difficult."

"Yes. I by now believe that he is simply not very good. Recently I had asked him to do something quite simple. It wasn't even urgent. But when I asked him two weeks later at the team meeting where he stood, he hadn't even started. That time, I really put him in his place."

"Obviously."

"He took it personally. I mean seriously. I am OK if someone makes a mistake. I wouldn't hold that against anyone. But at least you have to be open to feedback. If that is missing, I am totally losing trust in someone."

Whether one's own team operates internationally, has interfaces with other countries or people of different nationalities, sits together in the office side by side, most of us often interact with colleagues from different cultures or nationalities.

Intercultural collaboration is valuable — but it can be difficult

People from different cultural backgrounds not only have different perspectives and ideas, their values and the way they communicate also tend to vary and decisions are often taken on a different basis. That can regularly lead to misunderstandings and conflicts in a team, meaning that it does not reach its full potential. Understanding the norms that influence the worldview of different team members is a prerequisite to foreseeing and avoiding potential stumbling blocks.

Take this chapter's opening scene: Peter sees himself at best as the first among equals in the team, appreciates clear instructions and direct feedback, and has a rather rigid understanding of time. Shantanu on the other hand comes from a culture that honors older people and pays respect to superiors, in which harmony tends to be more important than being right, where confrontation is preferably avoided and criticism is certainly not practiced in front of others and only ever in strongly packaged form. A form in which Peter probably wouldn't even recognize it. Moreover, there is a completely different understanding of time.

How very differently people tick and what values are being upheld can already be seen in proverbs that reflect centuries-old beliefs. In China, children learn that they have two ears, two eyes, but only one mouth, and that this should be reflected in their behavior. Accordingly, the "loudest duck" in the flock is to be shot. In the USA, on the other hand, there are good reasons to draw attention to oneself, after all "the squeaky wheel" is the one that gets oiled. In Germany, this is seen similarly and "one does not put one's light under a bushel". That applies to boys, at least. "Girls who whistle, and chickens who crow," the vernacular also says, should have their "necks wrung in time". This is without question a rather radical procedure for dealing with unwanted behavior.

Thus, we virtually absorb with our mother's milk what behavior is desired and accepted when and by whom. This works perfectly as long as the people around us have the same value system. It becomes difficult when they are clearly different. Suddenly, behaviour and expectations no longer fit together and we are measured by standards that are not our own.

Although, for example, people from most Western cultures tend to rate their own abilities as above average, this is rarely the case with people from East Asia. Even in anonymous surveys they tend to be modest. Not because they lack self-confidence, but to fit in harmoniously with their environment. Unsurprisingly, this is not necessarily helpful during appraisal interviews and procedures, which are common in many international companies.

Although such aspects should have been widely known long ago, it is one of my most frequent experiences in international assessment centers: Participants from East Asian countries tend to fall only into the "also ran" category and are criticised for not asserting themselves in discussions and showing too little "bite". Instead, the extroverted candidates are hyped and nobody is disturbed by the fact that there was no indication that they could adapt their own style to different environments.

A systematic view of differences

The Dutchman Geert Hofstede was the first to set about systematically investigating national cultures and discovering commonalities and differences that influence cooperation. He describes national cultures in six dimensions: power distance, individualism and collectivism, masculinity and femininity, uncertainty avoidance, long and short term orientation as well as indulgence versus restraint (see table 10).[170]

Power Distance Index = PDI	PDI describes the relationship to hierarchy and status differences. A high power distance means that the unequal distribution of power is expected. People accept their social position without questioning it. Cultures with low power distances, on the other hand, are egalitarian – such as Denmark. There is a high power distance in many (East) Asian countries and in the Arab world.
Individualism versus Collectivism = IDV	In individualistic societies – the USA is extreme – self-determination and self-responsibility are important. In a collectivist society – like Indonesia – the social environment plays an important role and influences personal decisions. For mutual support, unconditional loyalty is expected.
Masculinity versus Femininity = MAS	Masculine societies are more competition-oriented, feminine more consensus-oriented. Typical masculine characteristics are considered to include success orientation, willingness to compete and self-confidence, feminine are caring, cooperation and modesty. A high MAS index points to a dominance of "typically male" values, such as those found in German-speaking countries. The situation is different in the "feminine" Netherlands.
Uncertainty Avoidance Index = UAI	It describes how much the members of a culture feel threatened by uncertain and unknown situations. Countries with a high degree of uncertainty avoidance – such as Belgium or France – rely on clear rules and guidelines. Unorthodox methods are not appreciated. Cultures with little uncertainty avoidance – such as Great Britain – take a relaxed view. Brexit may be a case in point.
Long Term Orientation = LTO	This dimension describes the temporal planning horizon of a society; cultures with a low index value – such as Brazil or Saudi Arabia – honor old traditions. It is important to save face and fulfil social duties; changes are viewed critically. Societies with a high index value – such as Hong Kong or China – are pragmatic and adapt to changing situations.

| Indulgence versus Restraint = IND | In compliant cultures – as in many Latin American countries – it is customary to reward oneself, enjoy life and have fun. Controlled cultures – for example in East Asia – follow strict social norms. |

Table 10: Six dimensions of national cultures according to Geert Hofstede[171]

Critics complain that such models encourage stereotypes and that it is important to treat each person as an individual rather than pigeonholing them. However, those who start from zero with every single acquaintance or – even worse – take their own culture as their benchmark, make life either extremely difficult or far too easy for themselves.

Models for intercultural cooperation provide a framework for clustering experiences. But they are not manuals for the smooth interaction with people from different cultures. Even if values and norms influence behavior, obviously not all people of the same nationality are the same. As with other personal characteristics, the different dimensions follow a Gaussian normal distribution (see figure 14). The apex defines what is described as "typical". However, those who feel well-prepared for the next intercultural encounter with a simple "Americans are egalitarian" or "Japanese are very hierarchical" will hardly achieve their goals.

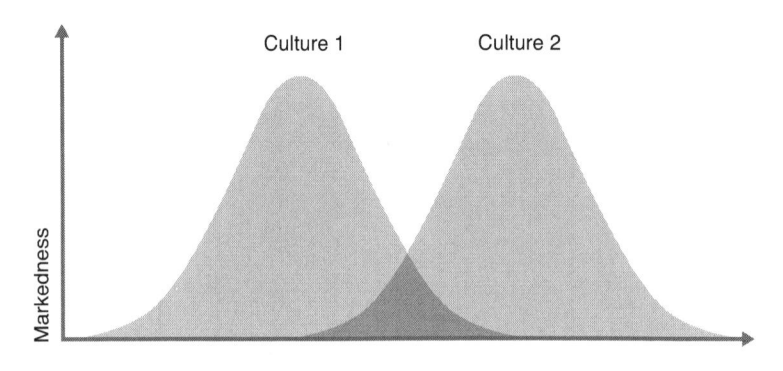

Figure 14: Not all people demonstrate behavior that is "typical" for their culture. Behavior follows a Gaussian normal distribution[172].

Erin Meyer, a professor at INSEAD Business School, has identified eight areas where cultural differences influence our interactions. They form the basis of her culture map, a very tangible model with a high practical relevance.[173]

Communicating

The grouping of the communication style takes place along the axis "low or high context". In context-poor cultures, little or no background knowledge is required to understand a message. "Good" communication is precise, simple and direct. Instructions are also given in writing to avoid misunderstandings. This is quite different in context-rich cultures, where messages are multi-layered. Little is expressed directly; instead, due to the shared context, it is assumed that the interlocutors also read between the lines. A nice example was recently provided by a Dutch friend (context poor), whose French boss (relatively context rich) asked her if she would like to take on a particular project. She felt perfectly at ease giving a straightforwardly negative answer to the question and was surprised at her boss's annoyance. "Why didn't he just say what he wanted straight up?", she still complains.

Evaluating

While there is agreement across cultures that feedback should be constructive, there are significant differences in the assessment of what this means. Here the preference varied between "clear and direct" on the one hand and "diplomatic" on the other. I'll never forget how a participant from Israel (extremely direct) was told after a role play by a British observer (much more diplomatic), that his dealings with the other participants had been extremely direct, and now he reacted visibly pleased and indeed flattered.

Persuading

This is about how I try to convince others and what I find convincing, which is strongly influenced by a country's culture and the factors – such as philosophy and religion – that influence it. The scale distinguishes between the principle and the application. While Germans tend to start with the facts that logically lead to a result (deductive), Americans and Britons are more likely to be persuaded if one begins with the conclusion and only then presents the data that lead to this recommendation (inductive).

Leading

This area is about power distance, i.e. about respect and esteem for authorities, about egalitarian or hierarchical cultures. This topic – together with the style of communication and how decisions are made – forms the focus of the next chapter.

Deciding

This dimension takes into account the extent to which people in different cultures seek consensus. While in egalitarian cultures decisions are usually made more democratically and top-down in hierarchical ones, there are some deviations from the norm. In the egalitarian USA, superiors are more likely to make a call that may also differ from group opinion. In the clearly more hierarchical German work culture, on the other hand, consensus has a higher significance. More on this in Chapter 12.

Trusting

A distinction is made between cognitive (from the head) and affective (from the gut) trust. In task-related cultures, trust is built up over time through positive (work) experiences that prove that someone deserves trust. In relational cultures, trust is based on a strong emotional connection and shared personal experiences.

Disagreeing

Cultures differ fundamentally as to how productive they judge arguments and confrontation to be for teams or organizations. This axis shows the acceptance of open confrontation and whether it is perceived as helpful or obstructive for cooperation. A Chinese friend, for example, warned me about this with regard to her compatriots. When a colleague says he is going to think about something, I needn't expect to hear from him again.

Planning

Whether appointments are perceived as binding or at best as a rough guideline is another aspect that has a considerable influence on cooperation. Correspondingly, this axis indicates whether a structured, linear working approach predominates or whether the approach is largely flexible and reactive.

In overview this looks like shown in figure 15.

Determining one's personal position

The starting point for a better intercultural understanding is always a better understanding of myself. Where do I find myself on the different axes? What is important to me, what drives me crazy? Where did I grow up and what influence does this have on my value system?

Often it is difficult for us ourselves to recognize typical behavior for our culture. Obviously, the differences are enormous. We notice this practically every day with our friends and acquaintances. Additionally, we might hesitate to see ourselves as examples of our own culture. Famous German virtues – punctuality and diligence? That can't possibly be me.

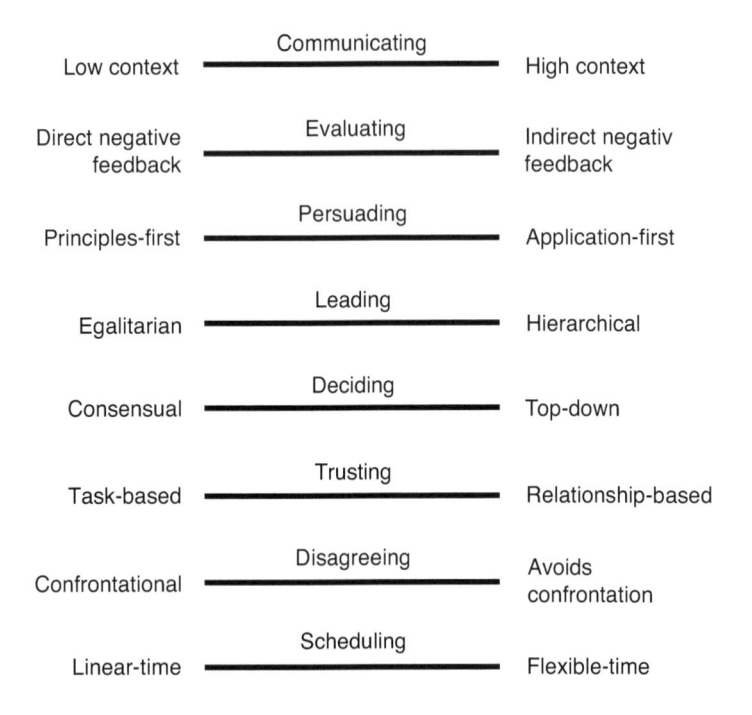

	Communicating	
Low context	———————	High context
Direct negative feedback	Evaluating ———————	Indirect negativ feedback
Principles-first	Persuading ———————	Application-first
Egalitarian	Leading ———————	Hierarchical
Consensual	Deciding ———————	Top-down
Task-based	Trusting ———————	Relationship-based
Confrontational	Disagreeing ———————	Avoids confrontation
Linear-time	Scheduling ———————	Flexible-time

Figure 15: Culture Map according to Erin Meyer

A parable offers an explanation: An old fish meets two young ones. Says the old one: "Lovely water today". The two others nod at him in a friendly manner. "What is water?", one of them asks after some thought. This is because culture is like privileges: Our own remains invisible to us because it defines our normality – the "usual" behavior, the "natural" reaction. Our own culture is the yardstick for what we experience as strange, as exaggerated, as unnecessary, or for behavior that we simply do not understand or to which we are blind.

However, those who make themselves aware of the different dimensions and gain an understanding of where they and others are located on the axes get a good idea of possible points of conflict in the team and what they can result from. It is important to bear in mind that the view of other cultures is influenced by what is "normal" for us. Whether Germans are hierarchical or egalitarian is a question people from Denmark (much more egalitarian) and Japan (much more hierarchical) will answer very differently. On the other hand, they will quickly agree that they are direct and value a strict adherence to schedule.

I experienced the importance of the personal perspective in intercultural trainings in the Netherlands particularly clearly. They were intended to help improve cooperation between local IT teams and the extended workbench in India. In the process, the Dutch managers regularly complained about the insufficient adherence to deadlines and the annoying laissez-faire attitude of their Indian counterparts. This always made me feel a slight malicious delight. After all, I myself regularly had exactly the same impression when working together with colleagues from the Netherlands.

But much more important than "serves you right" is another message: where I am on one of the eight axes defines how I experience another culture. Whether it appears to me, for example, as rigid and inflexible or chaotic and unreliable. While from an Indian perspective the Netherlands has a culture that almost pedantically sticks to agreements once made, without considering any aspects that might influence the planning, from my point of view its reliability sometimes left a lot to be desired. That is despite the fact that I would never call myself particularly German!

Successful with international teams

Trust is crucial for successful cooperation. It is the prerequisite for being fully involved, to have fun and energy and to also get tricky tasks solved. Because of different values and norms, building this trust in multicultural teams is a particular challenge.

A basic prerequisite is a common goal and the necessary information and tools to work successfully towards it. It is also important to create transparency for existing differences and for the frictions, conflicts and injuries that can arise from them. This creates the basis for agreeing on clear rules for cooperation and dealing with each other. Since everyone regularly operates outside their "standard mode", it is important to reaffirm agreements again and again. Good communication is a critical factor for success. Only communication can address the different needs for information and make transparent for all what needs to be done and by whom to achieve shared goals. Regular conference calls and video meetings, updates by email and one-on-one conversations can help overcome boundaries if participants are in different locations.

At the same time, regular and timely communication enables all participants to prepare for appointments appropriately. This is particularly important for those who are not involved in day-to-day communication, and who therefore often lack information that has simply been shared in passing. And it addresses the needs of people in less individualistic cultures who need to coordinate with others.

For many cultures, shared experiences – instead of just smooth cooperation – create the basis for trust. Therefore it is important to plan for this. If you don't just report on the status of your work, but also find opportunities to talk about non-occupational interests and hobbies, as well as about what's bothering you privately at the moment, you can identify similarities and establish personal relationships more easily. Especially in the initial phase of a collaboration – or when the team composition changes – it is important to build such intercultural bridges.

International teams that are spread across locations are helped by the right technology. It doesn't always have to be the best or the newest. Much more important is that all participants feel comfortable with the platform and with using it. It is important to ensure a reasonable balance between "fast and uncomplicated" and the quality of the interaction. While email and chat features are convenient, they are also ideal for misunderstandings and escalation. Video platforms, on the other hand, offer far more clues as to whether information is received correctly and make it possible to address ambiguities directly and thus avoid conflicts.

Tips for intercultural cooperation

Get acquainted with your own culture and that of your team members. There are numerous tools and books that give a good impression of where potential cultural misunderstandings lurk. www.hofstede-insights.com, for example, offers a free "country comparision tool" with which you can compare cultures that are particularly relevant to you.

Don't pigeonhole anyone. Origin is just one factor that influences our style and actions. In addition, influences that someone has experienced can look completely different than we suspect. Meet people with an open mind and avoid preconceived notions.

Make yourself aware of the strengths of different approaches. Learn about the advantages of other styles instead of simply perceiving them as "different". This creates appreciation and respect.

Practice intercultural fluency. To convey the same message and achieve the same result, you need to be responsive to others. Practice adapting your style to meet different needs and expectations.

Plan for different needs. Unlike in Western countries, where people are often willing to shoot from the hip and express themselves on anything at almost any time, less individualistic cultures require more coordination. Provide early information about topics and contents of meetings in order to give time for preparation and coordination with others.

Get to know target cultures. If you deal a lot with people of a certain culture, use the opportunity to get to know them. Visit the country and try to experience the daily realities.

Chapter 12
That's never going to work!

How to be successful with international teams

The last "Goodbye", "Thank you" and "Speak soon" had hardly faded away, when a tumult broke out in the conference room. During the conference call, there were too many different ideas on how to proceed and the timetable for the project. Only Shantanu sat there and remained silent.

"These Americans are crazy! Their ideas are completely unrealistic!"

"Exactly! Always saying that one feels honored and proud to make a contribution and when it comes to making a difference, there's only discussion instead of delivery."

"The French are no better either. A friendly 'Oui, merci' and as soon as they have hung up, they completely ignore all agreements and do what they like."

"Still better than the Spanish, they missed the call altogether."

"And the Chinese! Sitting together in front of the phone and then no one will speak anyway."

"It's no wonder that the projects are falling apart. First nobody says anything, then nobody knew anything and finally nobody was responsible ."

"Fortunately you found clear words there, Peter. They always seem to rely on us being the well-behaved, super-organized Germans and getting things done in the end."

International projects are a great opportunity to increase your visibility and to position yourself for larger tasks. Unfortunately, they offer almost as good an opportunity to maneuver yourself into a blind alley or to get thrown off any lists of an organization's key talents. Being German, I sometimes get the impression that my fellow nationals do that particularly well due to "typically German" preferences and style. However, it's probably just that I'm particularly aware of this, that I recognize the signs very clearly but also know what positive intentions are hidden behind a behavior that sometimes goes down quite differently with others.

Clash of cultures

It is often typical cultural aspects that, cause misunderstandings and unnecessary friction.

First, there are the different communication styles and preferences, and the question of how acceptable it is to openly address conflicts. In addition, there are very different ideas about the importance of rank and status, and how respectfully we treat people who are above us in the hierarchy. And finally, how quickly decisions are made and how binding they are.

As if all this were not complicated enough already, language often additionally hinders the exchange. Discussions usually take place in English and participants cannot express themselves as precisely and with as much nuance as in their mother tongue. All this leads to an extremely confusing mixture, that we will examine in this chapter.

Communication

Let's start with communication and two reasons we don't understand each other: our language styles are not necessarily compatible and often, we don't give each other sufficient space.

Voice frequency

In a conversation or discussion, the frequency of speech varies enormously across cultures (see figure 16). While in Anglo-Saxon languages, for example, arguments are exchanged in relatively quick succession – the end of a statement is taken as a signal by the other person to start with his or her own statement – things are quite different elsewhere. In Asia, it is rude to talk as soon as the other person has finished. The pace of exchange is slower, and it is considered a sign of respect to process what has just been said before someone makes a statement. In Romanic languages, such a pause in conversation is unthinkable. It would signal that people have nothing to say to each other and is perceived as embarrassing. Anyone who generally lets their own "feel-good factor" dictate the flow of speech loses out. They may not be able to get a word in or miss important information and arguments because they don't leave enough room for others to address them.

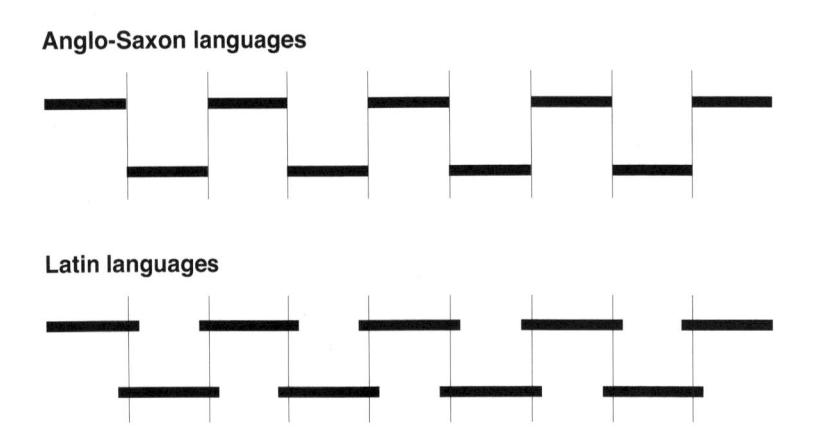

Anglo-Saxon languages

Latin languages

Asian languages

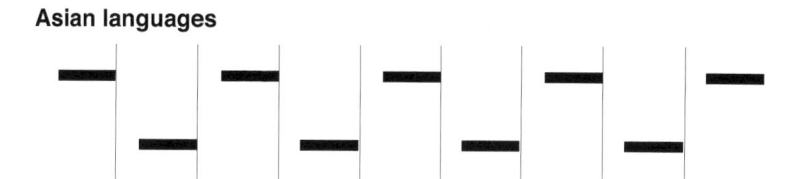

Figure 16: Different languages follow completely different patterns[174]

Direct and indirect communication

Even if all participants succeed in getting their say, this is only the first step towards successful communication. Because the way we speak differs fundamentally. In the last chapter I talked about communication with a high or low context and how we handle criticism and negative feedback – immediate and very direct or especially face-saving.

A higher level of education does not make things any easier. Instead, the challenges become even greater. The higher their level of education and position, the more closely people tend to get to the ideal of their culture as they speak. Top (context-poor) US leaders have deeply internalized rules such as "say what you are about to say, say it and say what you have just said". Probably, they even recapitulate their arguments by e-mail afterwards. In Japan, which is at the opposite end of the context scale, this approach is perceived as primitive, as a way of talking that is not fit even for addressing a child and obviously strongly questions someone's intelligence.

But it is even worse the other way round. While people from context-rich cultures might experience context-poor statements as flat and uncultured, their more sophisticated statements are often completely misunderstood. Like long-standing acquaintances or an old married couple, their language presupposes too many common values and experiences that are necessary to interpreting and classifying what has been said. However, if the common context is missing, the artfully packaged messages will not get through at all. Other than one would expect, the biggest misunderstandings are not between people at the opposite ends of the scale. Communication breaks down completely when people of different cultures with context-rich language meet. Then both try to read intensively between the lines, but tend to draw completely wrong conclusions, based on different experiences, as to what might be meant.

For intercultural teams, context-poor communication works better in principle, but because it can be uncomfortable depending on the culture, it is important that everyone agrees on it.

Discussion and feedback

The way in which discussions happen and criticism is expressed also differs fundamentally and offers a great deal of potential for conflicts within the team. Some cultures enjoy vigorous discussions and see them as an opportunity to exchange arguments or simply to test and develop ideas. For them, a decent discussion proves the strength of cohesion and the trust you place in each other. In "introverted cultures", on the other hand, consideration for the feelings of others has a special value that is reflected in communication norms. In China or Japan, for example, it would be unthinkable to offend someone in public and cause them to lose face. Even when it comes to important concerns, the feelings of others are always taken into consideration and included as a perspective.[175] Harmony can be more important than "being right", because of the fear that conflicts can damage the group.

To get an impression of very different preferences, you don't have to look far. Looking at both sides of the English Channel is enough (see table 11). For me, no one has ever again represented the typically British character as much as my colleague David, in his early 60s, and the perfect English gentleman. When we sat together on a team and were absolutely in agreement on the fundamental rejection of a plan, no one but ourselves would have noticed it. While I expressed my annoyance bluntly and frightened people from more indirect and obliging cultures, his words of displeasure came with mild irony that most of the international team did not even recognize.

What the British say	What the British mean	What Germans understand	What Germans would say
I would suggest you ...	Take care of it.	I can decide whether I want to take that into account.	Take care of it.
Your idea is original.	What a completely ridiculous idea.	Out of the box! People will like it.	What a completely ridiculous idea.
I am sure it was me ...	How did you ever think of anything this stupid?	It is your fault and you are sorry.	How did you ever think of anything this stupid?
I was a little bit disappointed that you ...	I am mad as hell.	It doesn't really matter.	I am mad as hell.
By the way ...	What this is really about ...	This does not really matter.	What this is really about ...

Table 11: Intercultural communication gives ample room for misunderstandings[176]

In Germany it is quite common to give negative feedback directly to people – "after all, it's about the thing and not the person". The US-Americans, for example, prefer a different approach, not to mention East Asian countries. In addition, German culture is very open to conflicts. But anyone who is convinced that having it all out will clear the air often experiences a nasty surprise in an international context. Like an axe in a forest, they will leave a trail of devastation and nasty injuries.

The actors are often not even aware of the effect of their own behavior because indirect feedback, such as the advice to perhaps reconsider one's own behavior, is at best understood as a friendly recommendation that does not deserve greater attention. Anyone who tells others "you are totally wrong", "I see it completely differently" or "not at all" tends to ignore more subtle hints. This becomes a problem at the latest when projects don't run smoothly. Then interpersonal conflicts create additional barriers and result in issues like important information not being shared.

This is especially true because participants regularly communicate in a foreign language and thus feel restricted in their abilities. Those who have a large vocabulary in their mother tongue and express themselves precisely in it often loose important soft skills when speaking "foreign". At the same time, it can be difficult to demonstrate one's own expertise, which is more likely to be expected behind a polished language. This, too, can be frustrating and lead to results that fall well short of the group's potential.

A recent study of teams with members from the USA and East Asia shows particularly clear evidence of the necessity of not simply "letting communication run its course". Without appropriate intervention, Americans spoke five times more often and almost ten times more. Only common rules create an acceptable balance: clear agreements as to who speaks when, and making use of open questions to invite everyone to share different perspectives. With such an inclusive approach, American team members expressed themselves only 1.5 times as often as those from China, Japan, Korea and Taiwan, and the proportion of speech was similar.[177]

Hierarchy

One important aspect of such an inclusive culture is understanding the meaning of status. Respect for the elderly and those who are higher up can easily silence employees working in hierarchical cultures. And even though generational change in China has affected expectations towards managers on the part of younger employees – like their Western peers – wanting a participatory management style[178], conditions there are still very far from what is common in Western countries.

In the early 1990s, I started my career at HP, a company in which everyone addressed each other by first name, which was very unusual in Germany at that time. Additionally, there were no separate offices; instead everyone worked in an open space environment. The PR department sat opposite the top management, and we were a decidedly cheerful group. So whenever our enthusiasm started to go overboard, Menno, Fritz or Rudi – the managing directors – would stick their heads over the screen and ask us whether we would mind being a little quieter. Even today I remember my bewilderment when I discovered a few years later at Alcatel that my assistant was sitting in an anteroom to shield me from others. Even at the end of the last millennium this struck me as a relic from a bygone age in view of my socialization.

The environment you live and work in shapes you, and it demands a considerable degree of rethinking to navigate a culture in which status has a completely different significance. This is why the increasing importance of agile organizational forms and flat hierarchies creates new hurdles in cooperation with important growth markets. Members from hierarchical cultures – where decisions are made "at the top" – often feel insecure about the changed role and fear losing status or even face in international teams if they follow their own norms.

Deciding

Hierarchy also plays a role in how decisions are made and by whom. The same applies to the preferred decision speed. Wanting to be fast helps to explain one of the most noticeable deviations: In the relatively egalitarian USA, decisions are often made top-down – and on the basis of minimal information. "Analytical paralysis" – being paralyzed by too long discussions – is despised, instead the focus is on action. This strategy, which was already used when the West of the USA was being conquered, is still practiced today and is increasingly becoming a successful export under the label "fail fast".

The immediate counterpart is Germany, which is actually more hierarchical, but simultaneously much more consensus-oriented. Very different labor laws, committees such as the supervisory boards, as well as worker co-determination have a strong influence on decision-making processes and fuel the desire to get it right the first time around. Half-baked ideas and guidelines are not compatible with this approach;

they are perceived as ill-considered and unprofessional and cause discussions to escalate. (see figure 17).

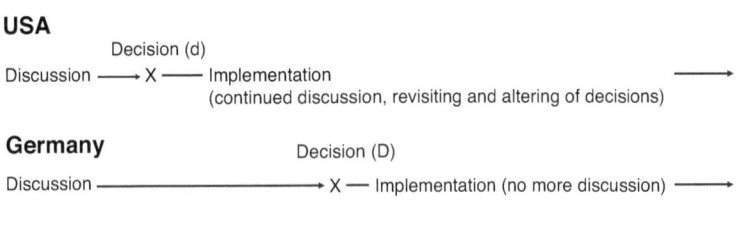

USA

Decision (d)
Discussion ⟶ X ⟶ Implementation ⟶
(continued discussion, revisiting and altering of decisions)

Germany

Decision (D)
Discussion ⟶ X ⟶ Implementation (no more discussion) ⟶

Figure 17: Decisions are not equally binding

One problem here is a fundamentally different conception of what a "decision" actually is. An acceptable basis from which to act – or a set of rules carved in stone that leads directly to the goal? Erin Meyer distinguishes here between a decision with a capital versus a lowercase "d".[179]

This different view and approach lead to fierce disputes in German-American cooperation (as well as many other countries with similar traditions and laws) because some people have no idea why there is endless talk instead of finally getting down to work, while others can hardly believe that weeks of work are wasted, because the firmly agreed approach is suddenly meaningless and everything discussed anew.

In order to successfully drive international projects forward, it is important to understand how agreement is reached and what has actually been agreed. This is to make sure that one is perceived neither as unbearably bureaucratic nor as completely chaotic. To be able to invest energy where it actually contributes to the result. To understand whether "fast" is considered evidence of determination or poor preparation. Whether an agreement is binding or just a plan and subject to further change.

This also means understanding how decisions are made and what meetings are actually about. Are they for making decisions and do they have a big or a small "D"? Are options discussed? Or are decisions being approved that were prepared long in advance so that all arguments are meaningless?

Tips for success in international projects

Be flexible. Meetings are only part of the decision-making process. Create other opportunities to identify and influence key stakeholders.

Adapt your style. Think about where you'd place yourself on the communications and conflict axes. Often it is worthwhile to ask colleagues from other cultures for their opinion. Adapt your style to be compatible with that of the people you are working with.

Find ways to hear different perspectives. Make it culturally acceptable to express a dissenting opinion. Ask participants to play the devil's advocate, or ask everyone to name pros and cons of different options or concerns they may have heard from others.

Agree on rules. As a team, agree on common ways of working. This includes rules for meetings, timely mailing of agendas, and minutes and action points that may be shared with other levels. Explain why this is necessary, even though in some cultures it can be seen as a sign of a lack of trust.

Use low-context communication. To prevent misunderstandings, intercultural teams need low-context communication. The same is also strongly recommended for any written communication and online forums. Anyone who tries to score with irony often reaps a storm of fury because common experiences and context are missing, making it impossible for others to read between the lines.

PART 5
WOMEN AND MEN

The last part of this book deals with how gender influences our experiences in the workplace, what effects it has on how we are perceived, what expectations are placed on us and what support we receive.

The focus on men and women is naturally too narrow. The days of binary gender assignments are over. There is a simple reason why I still concentrate on men and women in this part: available research. No other difference has been better investigated. And the basic recommendations will not change: show appreciation, find common ground and be open.

What awaits you in the next chapters?

Chapter 13, "I need to leave early today, the preschoolers are putting on a play", examines the two key criteria by which we judge people: warmth and competence. It explains why these traits are so important and how they affect how we think of men and women.

Gender also has a strong influence on what behaviors are expected and accepted of different people. Chapter 14, *"Don't blow your own trumpet"*, deals with the fact that the same behavior is evaluated completely differently and what possibilities there are to achieve common standards.

Chapter 15, *"Cat fight"*, finally gets to the bottom of the notion that women do not support each other. It explains how this perception came about and why it is so persistent. It also highlights the contribution that men can make to achieving change.

Chapter 13

I need to leave early today, the preschoolers are putting on a play

How warmth and competence impact our judgement

"Taking half the day off again?" Linda quickly looked back over her shoulder and rushed on towards the elevator, while Peter waved towards her in a friendly manner. She was definitely going to be late. There would be trouble at the preschool. At least she had met her deadline despite all interruptions and her data was correct. Of that she was certain.

"Mothers. I often feel sorry for them", Curt stood next to his boss. "Always on the run."

"And whether they're here or there – they're never fully present."

"My wife doesn't want to get back to work until the youngest is in schools and then only part-time."

"Same here. But I get it. Every family is different. I am happy to support Linda to make sure things work out."

"That's fabulous. By the way, I also need to leave early today. They are putting on a play at the preschool. And our youngest has a part in it."

"Congratulations! He must be excited – and you probably are, too!"

"Obviously. We practiced really hard. He's a tree."

"Wow! You must be really proud!"

Although Peter wants to be supportive of Linda, his comment is not helpful. While off-hand comments are often aimed at lightening the atmosphere, they also remind everyone of the existing norm – and that not all team members fully comply with them. Linda probably feels slightly guilty. Not just about her daughter and the kindergarten teacher, who have to wait because she desperately wanted to finish her work. But also towards work, because she might have left the impression that her dedication was not enough. Or she could be angry at her boss who apparently did not appreciate her efforts as much as they deserved. But it is not just in Linda's mind that unwanted thoughts could take root. Unconsciously the "usually only works half days" could stick with Peter and impact his judgement at the next performance review. Even more so since Linda's behavior probably is read differently from that of her colleagues. If she is not at her desk, people are likely to believe she is at home with her daughter. Men are supposed to be in meetings or visiting clients.[180]

We met Julia in the opening scene of Chapter 8. She has two small children and a husband working part-time. That didn't help with her career, because the leadership team did not want to burden her with a role that requires a lot of travel. The problem: → *gender stereotypes* are not just → *descriptive* i.e., impact our perception of what women and men are like. They also have → *prescriptive* elements, meaning that there are clear expectations of what people should be like.

This can mean that managers support women in being the mothers they want to be, at least according to the expectations of that manager. A woman's own preferences are not necessarily taken into account; in fact, she is often not even asked, because no one considers that she might have a different perspective. Alternatively, bosses want to protect her from having to turn down a position they don't consider suitable anyway.

Parents are confronted with different expectations

But it is not just mothers struggling with balancing career and family. Increasingly, fathers speak up. In Germany, 92 percent say that striking a balance is very important, but every second respondent struggles at times. Fathers only put limited faith in the support of their employers. Also, 38 percent fear financial consequences in case they take parental leave and one in three that it will have a negative impact on performance evaluations.[181] Researchers in the US found that their concerns are well justified. Employees seeking flexibility after having a child were given lower performance evaluations than those with traditional work arrangements.[182]

At the same time, flexible work arrangements hardly help: fathers who can independently plan their working time actually spend an hour less per week with their kids vs. fathers with fixed schedules. Instead they put in an additional 3.5 hours of overtime.[183] After all, prescriptive stereotypes also impact fathers. Whereas mothers are pressurized to leave on time to get home to their children, a new father is expected to exert himself all the more. After all, he now has a family to provide for.

Mothers are not only slowed down by typecasting, though. They also fall victim to the fact that two dimensions are key for our judgements of others: competence and warmth.[184] Warmth stands for aspects like morality, trustworthiness, sincerity, kindness, and friendliness. Competence relates to perceived ability to enact intent, i.e. efficacy, skill, creativity, confidence, and intelligence, and whether we are able to inspire respect.

Becoming a mother automatically increases warmth, but just as automatically she is perceived as less competent. The perception is that it is impossible for her to remain level-headed and on task in that situation. But while her allegedly lower competence impacts her ability to advance, higher warmth does nothing for her. The effect is considerably different for new fathers. They score higher on warmth with no negative effect on factors like efficacy or intelligence.[185] While it thus makes sense for mothers to "cover", e.g. not to mention any child-related activities or show off any baby photographs, men can benefit from the opposite strategy. If he is beaming with pride over the newborn this can positively affect his career.

Friend or Foe? And why does it matter?

There is a simple reason why warmth and competence are so important for our judgement of others. They are the simple answer to two very important questions:

- How do you relate to me? Are you friend or foe?
- Are you able to act upon your intentions? Can you hurt me?

Even if someone is hostile towards me, I can happily ignore those sentiments as long as that person does not have the ability – the competence – to act upon their intentions. Also, it is obviously better if we can actually benefit from the promised support of someone kind and friendly because they have what it takes to succeed.

Based on this warmth-competence model, you can easily map out some archetypes (figure 18):

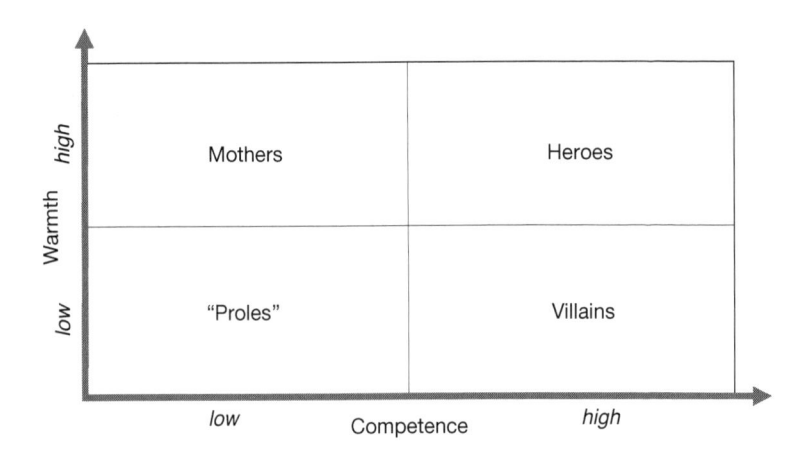

	low Competence	high Competence
high Warmth	Mothers	Heroes
low Warmth	"Proles"	Villains

Figure 18: It is not enough to be nice to be valued (based on the warmth-competence model by Amy J. C. Cuddy & all[186])

Gender stereotypes heavily impact our judgement – not only about mothers and fathers. Women are generally perceived as "warm"; men are considered "competent".

An analysis of 81,000 US-Army performance ratings illustrates this dilemma almost perfectly: While the performance of women and men was the same based on objective indicators, their subjective assessments differed considerably. The most commonly used positive term to describe women was compassionate, whereas for men it was analytical, followed by terms like competent, athletic and dependable. Women on the other hand were described as enthusiastic, energetic and organized, adjectives – all but the last – that are more reminiscent of Goofy (likeable, but not at all competent), than descriptions of someone you'd want to trust your life with.[187]

Different expectations create a dilemma for women

Many studies show that the expectation for women to be friendly and kind creates barriers to their advancement. "What is really going on, as peer reviewed studies continually find, is that high-achieving women experience social backlash because their very success – and specifically the behaviors that created that success – violates our expectations about how women are supposed to behave", summarizes Marianne Cooper, a sociologist at Stanford University. "Women are expected to be nice, warm, friendly, and nurturing. Thus, if a woman acts assertively or competitively, if she pushes her team to perform, if she exhibits decisive and forceful leadership, she is deviating from the social script that dictates how she 'should' behave. By violating beliefs about what women are like, successful women elicit pushback from others for being insufficiently feminine and too masculine."[188]

OK, you might think. Difficult, but not inconceivable. In that case she can develop her very own leadership style, try to be a little bit more obliging, rely on consensus and achieve her goals by being diplomatic. But that doesn't work too well either. If women are not decisive and taking a strong stand at times, their leadership ability is often questioned. They find themselves in a Catch-22 situation and lose no matter what they do. "I was routinely referred to as either a 'bimbo' or a 'bitch' – too soft or too hard, and presumptuous, besides",[189] remembers ex-HP CEO Carly Fiorina, touching on a theme that will resurface in Chapter 15, "Cat fight".

Building trust

Let's first understand which insights and tips the warmth-competence model can give for your own leadership behaviour. What can you do to make sure you are valued and maybe even admired by members of your team? That doesn't just feel good. It has a direct impact on your ability to succeed. Because employees who trust their manager and value their competence are not just more satisfied with their jobs and feel less stressed. Such trust is also a prerequisite to ensure that the increasingly widespread "stretch targets" – higher and more ambitious goals – actually lead to better results.[190]

Most people decide to demonstrate strength and competence in order to support their leadership ambitions. But that's not a good strategy. Increasingly, research demonstrates that it makes more sense to initially show warmth if you want to influence and lead.[191]

Let's take a second look at the warmth-competence matrix (figure 19) to understand why. It illustrates how our perception of different people impacts our feelings and behaviors.[192] Generally, people with high competence have high status. But only those who are likeable, who show appreciation for others, can count on our lasting admiration and support. Cold fish on the other hand are met with jealousy and envy. There is opportunistic collaboration at best, or we try to actively undermine them.[193]

An analysis of Fortune 500 companies shows how the perception of CEOs impacts the probability that they will become a target for their competitors. Researchers reviewed videos of CEOs and evaluated their appearance. CEOs who demonstrated a lack of warmth were more likely to be attacked regarding price, products, marketing and expansion.

Those that also appeared submissive (low competence) were faced with assaults even more often than provocative (high competence) leaders[194]

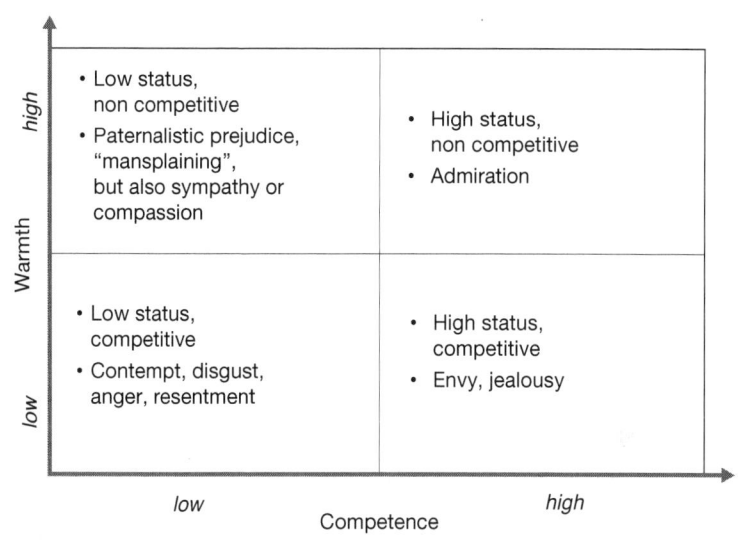

	low Competence	high Competence
Warmth high	• Low status, non competitive • Paternalistic prejudice, "mansplaining", but also sympathy or compassion	• High status, non competitive • Admiration
Warmth low	• Low status, competitive • Contempt, disgust, anger, resentment	• High status, competitive • Envy, jealousy

Figure 19: Strong collaboration requires trust[195]

What does that mean for personal interactions?

(Prospective) leaders who try to go strong, to demonstrate strength before trust is established, trigger fears regarding their intentions – whether they will be celebrating success together or pushing someone in front of a bus should the opportunity arise.

That does not help a leader to be effective. "Most people assume it is possible to be an effective leader without being likable. That is technically true, however you may not like the odds", says Jack Zenger. "We have calculated the probability as 0.052 percent. In a study of 51,836 leaders, we identified 27 who were rated at the bottom quartile in likability but were in the top quartile for overall leadership effectiveness. That equates to approximately 1 in 2000 cases that a boss who is highly unlikable appears in the top quartile of overall effectiveness."[196]

So, what to do to build trust?

There is whole range of measures that help increase warmth and improve relationships.

- **Meet others with interest.** Use non-verbal signals to demonstrate connection. Making eye contact, nodding and smiling are indicators of warmth. Showing other people that you are happy to see them and interested in what they have to say. Listening actively and following up with questions. Rather than focusing on your next response, really listening with the goal to truly understand.
- **Ask rather than speculate.** Discuss their priorities with team members and how they envision their career rather than speculating based on your own wishes and the way you live. Even if some career options might not work out, being asked is an important sign of trust. Accept a "no" and use it as basis to continue discussing alternatives rather than excluding individuals from development opportunities.
- **Make yourself vulnerable.** Share about yourself and experiences you have had – within reasonable boundaries. Talk about things that matter to you, that have had an impact and made you who you are. Share anecdotes that represent what you are *talking* about. If you open up, you will also learn more about others. That creates the basis for familiarity and trust to grow.
- **Ask for help.** Admit if you feel uncomfortable in a given situation or if you are not sure that you can read it correctly. Invite others to provide feedback, show that you care and act upon it.
- **Be empathetic.** Try to put yourself in somebody else's shoes. Discover what you have in common. What is happening for them? What are their hopes, wishes and concerns?
- **Show that you understand their concerns and take them seriously.** Offer compassion and sympathy even if you are not responsible for a given situation.

Women do that regularly. They apologize even if someone else made a mistake or ran into them. Often, they are criticized for that behavior. It is seen as weakness. But they are neither misreading the situation nor trying to make themselves small. Instead they signal to their counterpart that it is OK, that they are not angry with them or upset by their behavior and that the relationship won't suffer.[197]

Instead of criticizing their behavior, men might actually want to copy it. In one experiment, subjects were asked to go borrow the phone of a stranger in bad weather. Those who started their request with "I am sorry about the rain" succeeded 5 times more often.[198]

Tips to make each other's lives easier

<u>Focus initially on being liked vs. respected.</u> To establish yourself as a leader, it is smart to show warmth first, in order to build trust. On this basis you can demonstrate your competence to build your position.

<u>Remember that fathers are parents, too.</u> It is not just women who get into difficulties because they are almost automatically considered more interested in their children. Men wanting to be actively involved in parenting are often excluded from company offerings that are standard for mothers. That is not just unfair. It also preserves traditional views of family and gender stereotypes.

<u>Hold back with comments.</u> Even well-meaning comments about the behavior of team members can come across all wrong and create a very different effect from that intended. Remarks comparing the situation in your own family with that of others have a huge chance of backfiring.

Chapter 14

Don't blow your own trumpet

How our expectations impact our judgement

"And then I said: 'Now we are in agreement'", Yasmin was brimming with enthusiasm.

"Well, he really isn't a difficult customer. Anyone could have done that," Kurt objected.

"That's not true at all. We have been trying for quite a long time …"

"Do you want to get emotional now?"

"I'm not, but …"

"Come on, Yasmin, let someone else have their say."

"She can't help herself. Did you know that? Women speak more than three times as much as men."

"That's the disadvantage of women on the team. We men really have to stand together to get a chance to speak."

Although the myth survives that women talk way more than men, scientific studies do not support it. In an experiment with 400 students, for example, in which a digital device recorded what was happening every

12.5 minutes for 30 seconds over a long period of time, there were no significant differences between genders. While women spoke an average of 16,215 words, men spoke an average of 15,669. The most striking difference? For men, the distribution was considerably broader. While the quietest man only managed about 500 words during the course of the day, the most talkative one reached an impressive 47,000. Linguistics professor Mark Liberman of the University of Pennsylvania speculates that the legend of talkative women was invented by a marriage counselor "as a sort of parable for couples with certain communication problems, and others have picked it up and spread it, while modulating the numbers to suit their tastes."[199]

Men speak much more at work

While there are no major distinctions in everyday life, research finds that the proportion of men and women speaking in a professional context and in meetings is fundamentally different. In a linguistics forum, for example, comments by men were on average twice as long as those by women. The same was true for faculty meetings, researchers found when listening to recordings: with one exception the participating men spoke more often and generally longer. The longest comment of a woman was shorter than the shortest of any of the participating men. Also, while men in higher positions or when they feel more powerful take up considerably more time, such a correlation is not measurable in women.[200]

Men's opportunities for holding forth at length are due, among other things, to the fact that women are more often interrupted. When this happens, they tend to leave the field to their colleagues. When men experience the same thing, they tend to react differently. Instead of stopping, they usually finish their point.[201]

One of the reasons why women hold themselves back and don't "talk over others" is the fear of coming across as "too aggressive", of violating gender stereotypes and of being punished for it. The concern is certainly not unfounded. Feedback for women is all too often about their style of communication, and they are three times more likely to be told that they are too aggressive.[202]

Even if they negotiate, they are more easily criticized. Women who seek promotion are 30 percent more likely than men to be judged "intimidating", "obstinate" or "bossy" – and indeed 67 percent more so than women who do not negotiate.[203]

These fears make it easy for men to take up the space they want. It is like on an airplane, where many prefer to sit next to women, because they also tend to give up the armrests more easily. As a result, some men – mostly unconsciously – identify women as the easier target when they want to be heard in a meeting.[204]

A reason why it can seem acceptable to interrupt a woman's remarks: Their contribution to the group result is often overlooked or underestimated. So the cost of interrupting them may seem lower. In one experiment, jurors of a teamwork project were asked to assess the competence of the different participants, their influence on the result as well as their leadership behavior. Those who only knew the overall outcomes generally underestimated the role of the women involved. Only if her contribution was transparent or the judges were informed that she had consistently delivered positive performance in other projects did a woman's assessment catch up with that of the men.[205]

When being female or friendly becomes a barrier

The fact that expertise does not help women is also shown by an exercise in which it was necessary to escape from a bush fire. Such a task is considered to be classically "male", although the experiment showed no differences between the results of women and men. In the run-up to the experiment, everyone was left to decide individually what equipment offered the highest chances of survival. Those whose assessment best corresponded with that of people who actually knew what to do in such a situation were then assigned to different groups as experts. Irrespective of the personal outcome, women were generally perceived as less competent, and they hardly managed to influence the group. Their recommendations were wiped off the table and they were personally disqualified. Teams with female experts were correspondingly worse off than those led by a man. But while the women were clearly aware of their lack of impact, men did not have any doubts: whether expert or not, they were equally convinced that they had made a significant contribution to the survival of the group.[206]

Men also showed exuberant self-confidence in another study, in which the participants themselves were to select a "manager" to represent the team in solving a math problem. His or her performance would then define the result for each group member. Everyone had experience with the kind of task at hand: they had already solved a comparable one 15 months before. The participants had five minutes to decide who should represent them – and mostly selected a man as their leader. The reason? Past results formed an important basis for their choice, and the men had apparently performed better. Unfortunately, they overestimated their results by about 30 percent. And while the actual result was indeed a good indicator of competence, this did not apply to the inflated self-assessment. Although it helped men to be selected as leaders, it probably came at considerable cost for the group.[207]

The more "male" a topic is perceived to be, the more difficult it becomes for women to be taken seriously and to stand up for their ideas. If the gender of the participants is unknown in a discussion, women and men usually participate equally, and their contributions are similarly appreciated by the others. If they are recognizable as women, this changes – especially if they are the only one with a group of male interlocutors. It is enough to be perceived as female to evoke negative reactions. That's why nice men fall victim to this as well: in an analysis of chat conversations, friendly comments were generally attributed to women. Anyone who came across as negative or critical was automatically considered to be a man. Ideas from nice people – including men – were dismissed as less relevant regardless of their quality.[208]

Such unfair headwind is not without consequences. If the competence of women is regularly questioned, this can become a self-fulfilling prophecy. They lose interest in making a contribution, lose self-confidence and censor themselves. The fact that they become less visible is then regarded as proof that – as always assumed – it is a "male domain" in which women simply have nothing to contribute. Gender stereotypes thus solidify and groups do not reach their full potential.[209]

While companies complain about the low share of women in MINT (Mathematics, Informatics, Natural Sciences and Technology) disciplines, and try to get young girls excited in them in order to address the problem at least in the medium term, women are leaving the sector in droves. A research based on a longitudinal study by the U.S. Bureau of Labor Statistics shows that within 12 years half of women in technical roles – especially in engineering and IT – gave up their jobs and are reorienting themselves towards other fields.[210] The main reasons for this were dissatisfaction with the job and the conviction that moving to a different field was the only way to make it to the next level.

Different standards create barriers for women

At the same time, women struggle with additional inequities and unequal standards. While men tend to be promoted based on their potential, women are less likely to be considered "ready" and have to prove their suitability beyond any doubt before they are given the chance of a comparable position. Increasingly, they are drawing conclusions from this. A major German bank found that women did not leave the company – as initially assumed – because they were striving for a better work-life balance. Instead, they took on positions with the competition that their old employer had denied them.[211]

Vague concepts also bring down women. Not only are they seen as "warm" rather than "competent" and thus contradict traditional ideas of a "leader", but terms such as "executive presence" and "showing leadership" often also stand in their way because these terms are seldom clearly defined. What is actually meant, how it shows and what it is supposed to achieve. That's why promising candidates can easily be excluded from key assignments, development opportunities and larger roles even though they have the necessary skills.

In addition, women's achievements are often attributed to luck or to them simply having had more time to dedicate to a task rather than their abilities.[212] But when things go wrong, they are viewed more critically than their male counterparts. While his mistake could have happened to anyone, she simply messed it up. And a weak performance or a bad decision has far greater consequences for her. They are perceived as symptomatic – the ultimate proof that she hasn't got what it takes. And – thanks to stereotypical perception – her case also raises doubts about the qualifications of other women.[213]

The fact that women are less likely to be considered to have the proper qualifications is also due to the fact that these are often subject to change. Our mind has a pronounced ability to make things fit when they don't fit. In one experiment two candidates – a man and a woman – were to be evaluated for a stereotypical "male" job. The appraisers were informed that both training and work experience were important for the function. Of the applicants, one had more experience, the other had a higher formal qualification. Generally the man was preferred for the "man's job". The arguments were based on the matching facts. If he had more experience, this was rated higher. If he had higher academic qualifications, these were considered particularly important. But if decisive recruitment criteria were agreed before the gender of the applicants was visible, men and women had equal chances.[214]

But even if the selection is fair, the story is not over. Do you remember the "blind audition" that was so effective in helping women find their way into top orchestras? It wasn't until February 2019 that the Boston Symphony Orchestra reached an agreement with its first flutist in a court ruling. She earned less than the – male – leaders of all other instrument groups and about 25 percent less than the first oboe. This evidently had little to do with performance. Both being woodwinds, not only are the instruments relatively comparable, but also the tasks associated with the role. In addition, the oboist emphasized that the flutist was "my peer and equal, at least as worthy of the compensation that I receive as I am." What is particularly sad is that the case occurred in an orchestra that boasted of its efforts to be fair and was the first to introduce blind auditions.[215] Getting a job is just the first step. There remain many opportunities for discrimination afterwards.

Addressing change systematically

There's a lot to do, maybe more than expected. But we have it in our hands to make change happen. "Start by accepting that our minds are stubborn beasts", say Iris Bohnet, professor of Behavioral Economics at Harvard University. "It's very hard to eliminate our biases, but we can design organizations to make it easier for our biased minds to get things right."[216]

I have already introduced a whole series of instruments for fairer leadership in the past chapters: a procedure to support equal opportunities and comparability in job interviews; some models to visualize how I feel about different people and to check my view on them, like the different matrices or the tools for network analysis; strategies and tools to build trust and get to know people better; the Unconscious Bias Cheat Sheet, which helps to focus in times of information overload and to make fairer decisions.

Checklists are another helpful tool for approaching change systematically. Over the past few years, they have taken industry after industry by storm because they address a widespread difficulty. In the past, solving a problem often failed because we did not have the necessary knowledge or information. Today, a lack of information is often the least of our worries. Instead, we need to keep our bearings in the face of an overwhelming flood of data and impressions.

Checklists are not a particularly modern tool. They are extremely low-tech and without any gimmicks. But they have one unbeatable advantage: they help us to pause, reflect, and they keep us on course. Why? Because we can let ourselves think about what is important to us and what priorities we set before our minds switch to autopilot in the heat of battle.

Team checklists

Checklists for the team have another advantage. They help to stick to agreements and give members the power or permission to insist on the observance of agreements and rules, even if they would otherwise have avoided it.

How can such agreements be developed? Consider with your team what situations or behaviors lead to injustice. Do some people always arrive late for the team meeting and hold up others? Are there a few members that speak a lot and don't let anyone else speak or are others regularly interrupted? Does part of the team deliver reliably while others take a very relaxed attitude? If you know what needs to be changed, these five steps will take you there:[217]

1. Reflect together about any solutions someone might know that have worked in the past or in another context.
2. Define relevant behaviors on this basis. For example, if you want more people to speak, use a timer to keep statements short or agree to go around the table to see who wants to make a contribution. It is better to start with people who tend to express themselves more briefly. This also works – for most – as a primer for what is called for at the moment and defines a common standard.
3. Don't take on too much. First, concentrate on a maximum of five rules. Once they become the standard way of doing things you can take on new challenges.
4. Make a plan and define responsibilities.
5. Agree how to deal with rule violations.

An exemplary checklist for team meetings could look like this:

- To help everyone prepare, the agenda is available the day before the meeting with the necessary background materials.
- In the meeting, those responsible for the various topics ask all participants whether they have a contribution or comment. Everyone needs to respond, even just to say they don't have a contribution to make.

> - All team members are responsible for gathering feedback and ideas from others during the meeting.
> - Asking for opposing opinions is a general practice.
> - The order in which team members make comments is changed at each agenda item or meeting, so that each team member at times speaks their mind first or listens to others first.

Van Halen were famous for their checklists. They had precise specifications for every concert. Their contracts with concert promoters even contained a clause that a bowl of M&Ms had to be provided backstage, with all brown ones removed. If that condition was not met, they had the right to cancel the concert and the organizer still had to pay. What sounds like an absurd demand from a bunch of spoiled rock stars was a well-thought-out strategy. It was meant to be an easy way to verify that the band's requirements had been reliably met. "When I would walk backstage, if I saw a brown M&M in that bowl, well, we'd line-check the entire production", says David Lee Roth in his memoirs. "Guaranteed you're going to arrive at a technical error [...] Guaranteed you'd run into a problem".[218]

Checklists for people decisions

Personal checklists are especially worthwhile in situations where you tend to use shortcuts. When you have already experienced that mistakes or injustices have crept in, or at least cannot completely escape the feeling that they might have done so.

In the construction industry, a "clash detective" is used to bring different subsections together. This is software that checks whether there are any parts that don't fit together, meaning that someone has to take a close look and resolve the issue. Checklists give you the opportunity to develop your personal version of such a tool. To do so, consider in advance when mistakes tend to creep in, when your actions might collide with your values – on which occasions, with which people. Then plan for a stop, a pause, so that you don't stumble blindly into a situation, but approach it carefully. What are your triggers? What influences your behavior? What information do you potentially misinterpret? What might you overlook? Make a note of the things you want to concentrate on.

Not just unstructured interviews are an ideal breeding ground for prejudices. It also helps with assessments and other people decisions to define clear criteria and take a structured approach that applies to everyone. This helps to keep preferences and stereotypes at bay.

Make a note of the things you need to ensure in order to treat everyone fairly. For people assessments, for example, there must be clear agreements with everyone as to where their priorities lie. Obviously, this should be agreed and recorded as early as possible in the year. And should there be any changes during the year, these should also be discussed and recorded.

Define what you are looking for and what examples of the desired behavior might look like. Where candidates do not appear to meet the requirements, question the verdict. Write down examples. Confirm that you have applied the same standards to everyone and that there are no differences. Even if the decision is upheld, this provides you with the best prerequisites for giving detailed feedback to the disappointed candidates and agreeing on measures to address specific learning fields.

When writing assessments, make sure that they are comparable in form and content. That they have the same length, contain relevant examples, and that the tone and choice of words actually express what you want to convey. How important this is has been shown by an analysis of letters of recommendation. Those for women tended to be shorter than those for men. They were less complimentary and often included "doubt raisers" – apparent complements that left the recipient in doubt as to just how positive that feedback actually was. In addition, they mentioned their professional status less often, and the emphasized achievements followed gender stereotypes (she taught, he researched).[219]

Although they make life considerably easier, checklists are often dismissed. "I don't need them" or "I have experience", people often think. Anyone believing that could take flight captain Chesley B. Sullenberger III as a role model – Sully, the Hero of the Hudson. He had 20,000 hours of flying experience. But when the voice recorder from the cockpit was recovered after the emergency watering, they heard him and his co-pilot going systematically through their checklist.[220]

Tips for fairer decisions

Switch participants. Consider whether you would react differently to a person or a situation if those involved had different demographics. If they were of another gender, nationality, skin color or spoke with a different accent. If they were younger or older.

Define requirements. Make transparent what you expect. Success-promising behaviors can differ for different people. Define the goal instead of assuming that the same path will bring them all there.

Set the same standards. Ensure that you make the same demands of everyone. That you do not apply different standards or rules to different people in different ways. That the same requirements apply, regardless of who is being considered.

Rely more on your notes than on your memory. Make notes of the things you've been impressed with by team members you know less well. The things that come to mind automatically with those who are close to you will otherwise be more easily overlooked with the others.

Get help. Empower team members to help you ensure fairness, for example, by using checklists.

Chapter 15

Cat fight

Why it matters to step up and support others

"What's the matter with your Yasmin? She was always such a sunshine. Lately she seems irritable and curt."

"I have no idea. I asked Michaela from marketing to talk to her, woman to woman. But she refused. Had no time and didn't feel responsible."

"You hear that again and again. Once they've made it to the top, women don't tolerate another alongside them."

"I am extremely disappointed. How is anything expected to change if not even women support each other? It's no wonder then that there's only talk and nothing happens."

The idea of "Queen Bee Syndrome" still haunts the minds of people – the idea of women leaders who, like queen bees, prevent others from climbing the ladder. In conversations, everyone then can remember some cases in which women did not behave at all nicely towards other women. Subsequently, people shrug their shoulders slightly resigned, lean back and think that the situation is almost hopeless.

A dead concept keeps on twitching

That is not fair. The term "Queen Bee" was established in a study in 1974 – almost 50 years ago – and according to the researchers people missed the main point even then.[221] "I think people misunderstood our term", says Toby Jayaratne, Co-author of the study. "What they missed was the political climate and the sexist climate that created it." Instead the concept has mutated to become an outdated, sexist, negative stereotype. "There is never any 'King Rat' syndrome", adds research partner Carol Tavris. "An angry man is an angry man, but an angry woman is a 'bitch'".[222]

What led to this image being formed in the last century?

On the one hand, people who belong to an underrepresented group often see the need to distance themselves from other members. Because people "like them" don't actually get to the top in the company. You are familiar with the concept of "covering" from Chapter 2. Typical traits of the majority society are not only copied, but also pushed to the extreme so as not to create the impression that one has anything in common with the other members of one's own "group".[223] The fear of being suspected of favoritism when one woman stands up for another makes things even more difficult.[224]

Another reason is the experience that you yourself had to do more to be successful. In that case, higher standards are demanded from other women because they are obviously necessary for success. In addition, any mistakes they make could have potential consequences for yourself. If you belong to the same out-group, the behavior of one member can rub off on others.[225] Even today, some young women are still afraid that they will have fewer opportunities for development if a colleague becomes pregnant. After all, it reminds superiors that it might also happen to them.

And finally there is the so-called "tokenism". This is when a woman is appointed to a leadership position as an alibi – to make sure there is someone you can point to in a relaxed manner when there is criticism of an otherwise all male leadership team. If that "role" is filled, there is no room for other women in such cases. This can lead to her defending the acquired position with tooth and nail. "That scenario is unrealistic", one might say, "if they just tried, other women would be sure to follow". It is realistic, says science. In a study of the 1,500 largest companies in the USA over a period of 20 years, it became clear that it was easier for women to make it to the top if a woman ran the company. However, when a woman was appointed to the management team of a company with a male CEO, it was 50 percent less likely that another would follow.[226]

There is a similar trend today in the proportion of women on supervisory boards in Germany, albeit on a higher basis. After the introduction of a quota of 30 percent, the proportion of women had risen steadily. This trend stagnated once the statutory target had been reached and since then the proportion of women has even fallen slightly.[227] Apparently, in many companies there is still only room for as many women as strictly necessary. The "alibi logic" would also mean that the support among women would increase as their number in management positions grows. And indeed, studies have long since underscored this theory.[228] Women who have received support from others in the course of their careers are more inclined than their male colleagues to help those who come after them.

"There is a special place in hell for women who don't help other women", said former US foreign secretary Madeleine Albright, and most seem to share her perspective. In the end, says Carol Tavris, our behavior depends on the environment. It is a result of "how safe we feel at work. Does our work give us a chance to thrive? Or are we feeling thwarted at every step?".[229]

Stereotypes and prejudices continue to have an effect

Why is it that the idea still remains so ironclad? That so many people believe in cat fights?

An important aspect is the →*out-group homogeneity effect*. The behavior of a member of a foreign group – the out-group – is considered typical for everyone. There are so few women in top positions that the behavior of one often shapes the view of others. And of course there are women who get on your nerves, just as there are men like that.

Then there is the confirmation bias. It makes sure that you see what you expect. People (unconsciously) search for the information that confirms their assumption or notice it more often. Facts that do not correspond with a person's expectations, on the other hand, are accidentally but consistently overlooked. If I assume that there are queen bees, the corresponding behavior immediately catches my eye. "Aha", I think, "again!" The memory then blends seamlessly into my world view, and I am satisfied, because after all I always knew.

Another reason is – once again – gender stereotypes: the different expectations we have of women and men. It's about warmth and competence and about the minimum standards we set for different people. While it literally pays for men to support other people, the same behavior is simply assumed for women.[230] And if a woman is less friendly than expected, it really stands out. Any woman who gives critical feedback is considered less likeable and is less likely to be hired than men who say the exactly same thing.[231]

In other words, women remain stuck in the aforementioned dilemma of demonstrating "strong leadership" and being punished for it or being friendly and therefore not making progress.

Support boosts careers

The view that women are to blame themselves is quite convenient. It can be a practical excuse to explain why things are the way they are. And why men have nothing, absolutely nothing to do with the situation. The opposite is the case.

Elisabeth Kelan, Professor of Leadership and Organization at the University of Essex, has explored the role of male middle managers in creating an equitable workplace. She highlights that due to the very proportion of leadership roles they hold, men are central to changing gender relations at work by altering workplace practices. At the same time, she finds that many middle managers struggle to understand what gender-inclusive leadership actually can look like and how to display corresponding behaviors. Based on her research, she highlights four important actions men can take: celebrating and encouraging women to make sure that their skills don't go unnoticed; calling out bias; championing and defending gender initiatives (thus avoiding the meritocracy paradox), and challenging workplace practices.[232]

When men become active, careers can really take off. Employees who are supported by men earn more, are promoted more often and are more satisfied with the development of their careers. Women benefit even more because the backing helps them deal with the many hurdles that hinder their careers. They also feel greater psychological safety.[233] Unfortunately, women only have someone who supports their career about half as often as their male peers.[234]

Often two categories are distinguished: →*Mentoring and sponsoring*. The difference? "A mentor talks to you and a sponsor talks about you", as the organization Catalyst summarizes briefly.[235] While mentors act as sparring partners, discussing professional challenges and possible strategies with their mentees, a sponsor acts as an advocate in his or her environment. They help you to establish relevant contacts, get your name in the conversation and use their own reputation to support you.

Therefore it is hardly surprising that sponsorship – unlike mentoring – has a measurable influence on careers. Those who sponsor people believe in them and put their convictions into action. Unfortunately, more than two-thirds of them have the same gender and ethnicity as the people they support.[236] They are committed to people who are similar to them, with whom they feel comfortable and whom they meet at every turn.[237] #MeToo didn't make matters any easier. While some take the outcry as a convenient excuse, others feel troubled by the implications. Two of three men in senior leadership positions and 50 percent of female talent say they have concerns about entering into such a one-to-one relationship.[238] They are afraid that colleagues can or might want to assume that there is something completely different behind the joint meetings than professional support. But even in case you can understand that concern, the consequences are unfair. And it is not smart either.

Diversity and an inclusive culture are proven to deliver results, and they are important for the long-term success of any organization. Sponsorship is an extremely effective building block of leadership development. Those who exclude half the population from this support not only harm the company, but also fail to live up to their role as leaders and role models. Instead of giving in to fears, it is necessary to find ways to give the same support to different people. This is the only way to create equal opportunities for different employees.

Create a new "normal"

While sponsorship cannot be forced, it is important to create a climate in which this behavior is self-evident and there is transparency about who merits such attention and support. Sponsors must also act with absolute openness and make it clear that supporting talented employees of any gender is a key leadership task. Finally, it is necessary to clarify what such a relationship entails and according to what criteria people have access.

If such support is normal, if it is generally expected of managers instead of being an exception, this also removes the basis for potential rumors. "The evidence is really clear: if you have anxiety, there's only one treatment for that, that's exposure", says Brad Johnson, professor of psychology. "So you've got to lean in, you have to have more coffees and more lunches and more conversations with women and do it publicly. If that's your brand, if that's who you are in the workplace, people don't talk about that guy. He is just known for being a great collaborator, equally for men and women. And that's just not a guy who has to have anxiety."[239]

Anyone who gets involved doesn't benefit just the other person. Irrespective of the feeling that they are doing the right thing, white male managers who stand up for others are 11 percent more satisfied with their own career development than those who do not. For people of other ethnicities, the difference is as much as 24 percent.[240] One of the reasons might be that studies show that men who sponsor women get better performance reviews. Unfortunately, while the men are considered champions of diversity and rewarded for it, women tend to be judged more negatively. They are accused of favoring employees who are similar to them.[241] Thus, making it another reason why it is good for men to get actively engaged.

Moreover, the benefits are not unilateral. Instead, both profit from the exchange and new perspectives they receive. Men who enter the conversations openly and with curiosity also have the chance to learn more about the experiences that women have in the company. It is possible to expand one's own network and establish more connections to groups to which access was previously lacking. All in all, both parties stand to win in equal measure.

Getting started

There are a few basic rules that help to establish a successful sponsorship relationship:[242]

- **Same rules for all:** If you want to support people who are different from you, it is important to establish common rules with which both sides feel comfortable. When and where do the discussions take place? In the office or outside? During the day or in the evening? Discuss what worked in the past and build on it. Basically, however, the same rules should apply to all the people you support. If you meet those who are "like you" at dinner and "others" at the office in the morning, the results will probably be very different. Define the biggest common denominator that works for everyone. Make it the standard you'll always follow, even if it costs you a pleasant evening here and there.
- **Listen openly and with interest:** Be sure to have learning conversations (see Chapter 6), approaching the exchange with interest and openness, and avoiding speculation. Do not give tips or recommendations immediately. Listen and ask to understand what support is needed. Both parties should take the opportunity to learn and explore new perspectives.

- **Show vulnerability:** Talk about challenges you have faced in the past and are currently struggling with. Do not pretend to know everything. Share your own worries and fears, be vulnerable. This enables others to follow your example and talk openly about problems.
- **Acknowledge that experiences differ:** Those you talk to probably know that experiences are influenced by gender. Do not try to convince them otherwise. Discuss the possible effects, how to deal with different situations and how to help establish fair standards.
- **Take action:** Consider what you can do to help people achieve their goals. What opportunities exist in your area of responsibility to gain relevant experience and develop skills? Who else do you know who can offer relevant opportunities?
- **Give visibility:** Talk about the people you sponsor and their talents, as well as new challenges they need to develop their careers.
- **Gain broader support.** Talk to others about your experiences, the benefits you derive from your activities, and start a snowball effect.

Tips to boost the careers of others

Find out more. Find out what programs are available in your company and how you can get involved. If there is not much available, ask how you can help.

Get started right away. In personal interactions with people different from yourself, pay attention to what you can do for them. Don't say: "You're great, I want to sponsor you". That potentially comes across as weird. Instead, just go ahead and act. Make introductions and open doors when an opportunity arises. By sharing a common interest in success, a lasting dialog can develop and thus a more formal support.

Follow consistent standards. Create sponsoring relationships according to the same pattern. If you can't meet everyone over dinner, a glass of wine or an alcohol-free drink, don't do it at all. It is a sign of a culture that treats different people differently. This is not a thing you should support. It's better to use any free evenings that arise as a result to learn something new, to get involved in voluntary work or to indulge in hobbies. Unlike a nice evening, passionate, active leisure time leads to complete relaxation.[243]

AND NOW?

Over the last 15 chapters, we looked at the barriers different people face in their working environment and how they can be removed to create a level playing field. You read about specific situations or personal characteristics that shape our experiences. The final chapter examines what constitutes a workplace where employees are successful regardless of their personal demographics. It takes a look at the role managers play in creating an environment in which everyone gives their best.

Chapter 16
Fair Leadership

The fact that a workplace in which all employees can give their best is anything but self-evident is shown by a Gallup survey: only three out of ten employees in the USA believe that their opinion matters. If this figure were doubled, the rate of redundancies would fall by 27 percent, accidents by 40 percent and productivity would rise by 12 percent.[244]

Setting an example

Achieving such a change is up to you. Leaders are role models. Their behavior, the qualities they bring with them and how they interact with employees are responsible for 70 percent of the difference in team engagement.[245] They shape the standards in the team. They bring about change or stall it.

The example of Ignaz Semmelweis is a case in point. The doctor did not succeed in convincing his colleagues in elegant Vienna to wash their hands before delivering babies. The consequence? Women died of "childbed fever". Meanwhile, research has also come to understand why Semmelweis failed.

Two decisive aspects enable or prevent changes in groups. One is experience, when we discover that something works. That was clear in case of hand-washing. At Semmelweis' clinic, this habit led to "only" one in a hundred mothers dying after giving birth. In clinics where doctors also sometimes dissected someone between births, the death toll was one in ten.

The fact that the doctors nevertheless ignored the unambiguous evidence was due to the second motive which drives behavior and which had much more weight in this context: the herd instinct. To do what others in our group do. This is especially easy when it doesn't hurt one personally. It wasn't the doctors who died, it wasn't people in their circle of friends or relatives. Then it' s easy to "join in". It is simpler to hold on to the "tried and tested" than to risk social exclusion in one's own circle. You remember the micro-aggressions from Chapter 1?

In such cases a certain behavior is a signal. It demonstrates belonging. It shows which group – which clique – one belongs to. It makes one part of the in-group and allows them to benefit from all the advantages that that brings. The reason why hand-washing remained a neglected habit for so long was not the lack of evidence of efficacy. It was because Semmelweis did not understand or consider how social groups work.[246]

Belonging

Do you remember Kevin and Mandy and the students from the USA? In Chapter 7 I described how children improved their performance because they received more attention and appreciation. This is no different for adults. The problem is that we spend less time with people who are different, with whom we feel insecure or have reservations. We talk less to them, consult them less often and offer them less support. This is not only a problem in the one-on-one relationships, it is also a signal to other team members.

This is why it is so important to build trust with different people, in order to be a good leader for everyone. To address this strategically, the book has given you two important tools, the Competence Trust Matrix from Chapter 8 and the Relationship Map in Chapter 9. These allow you to reflect on the current quality of different relationships and plan how you can strengthen connections.

Chapter 4 dealt with the strength of diverse teams. They achieve better results, as already mentioned, because they avoid groupthink, offer more perspectives and because everyone makes a greater effort. But that is only half the truth. "If differences are not valued, you get friction but no reward", says Harvard Professor Robin J. Ely. In that case, the only impact on team performance will be negative.[247]

The feeling of being excluded and unfairly treated undermines trust and prevents people from giving their best. Because the mind is busy with other things which limits creativity and performance. Or because people don't share ideas, for fear that someone will take their butter from their bread, or because they are afraid that they won't be taken seriously or even laughed at.

Commitment to the team and performance beyond *"business as usual"* is only achieved by those who feel part of the group, to whom the big picture seems meaningful. This presupposes that everyone feels welcome and accepted as they are. That personal individuality is recognized and people experience appreciation for their abilities and for the perspectives they contribute instead of being judged or marginalized.[248]

The quality of a team is not measured by the opinion of a few individuals and certainly not by that of one's best friends. The advantages only come to bear when everyone feels equally respected and involved.

Successful Teams

How important common norms are in this process was established by a research team that investigated the intelligence of groups. It wanted to understand whether they might have a collective IQ higher than that of its members. They recruited people who had to solve very different tasks in small groups. In order to complete them successfully, cooperation was required.

This revealed a surprising phenomenon. Irrespective of the task, teams that were successful once usually had success again. Those who messed up tended to do so again and again. This is because what enabled success or caused failure was the way team members dealt with each other. The right norms increased the intelligence of a group, independent of its individual members.

While the different groups dealt with each other completely differently, they had two things in common: In successful teams all spoke more or less the same amount – even if perhaps in different phases of the discussion or during different tasks. In unsuccessful teams, on the other hand, there were just one or a few people who spoke most of the time. In addition, people in teams that solved tasks effectively interacted and paid attention to each other, including non-verbal signals. They noticed when someone felt excluded or insecure and then responded. Groups that failed more often, on the other hand, tended to be blind to the feelings of other team members.[249]

Psychological safety enables constructive conflicts

Psychological safety exists in a group when all members are convinced that they can take "interpersonal risks".[250] This enables them to show their own vulnerability without fear of a negative impact on their relationships, image, position or career. It makes it possible to admit uncertainties and mistakes, to learn and to ask for help. In this way, more can be achieved together.

Psychological safety does not mean glossing over real conflicts for the sake of fake harmony. Instead, it creates the basis for productive arguments and friction and thus for innovation and top performance. Without conflicts, groups lose their effectiveness. The supposed harmony exists only on the surface. Groupthink arises.

The opposite of conflict is usually not agreement, but apathy and disinterest. Teams that do not deal with substantial conflicts forget important aspects or are simply not aware of them. They fail to question assumptions and limitations or to develop different alternatives. Therefore they deliver on average a lower performance.[251]

In a "safe team" with friction, information is better used and problems are better understood. This leads to smarter and often unorthodox solutions. Such teams not only make better decisions, they also do so faster. Accordingly, organizations with an inclusive culture are six times more likely to be agile and innovative and eight times more likely to achieve better business results.[252]

An example? The designer Peter Skillman has carried out the so-called Marshmallow Design Challenge with many 100 participants worldwide. Teams of four were asked to build a tower out of spaghetti and carrying a marshmallow. The teams consisted of a wide variety of groups: engineers, lawyers, business administration students as well as CEOs. While they all mastered the problem very differently, one group beat them by far: kindergarten children. While the others were planning and discussing, trying – conspicuously cooperatively – to clarify or improve their position in the team or, alternatively, to blindly acknowledge the superiority of others, the children immediately got down to business. They didn't care about status; feedback was direct. They stood close together, saw mistakes and responded immediately. They took risks, experimented and built the highest tower of all. They were successful, not because they were smarter or better at planning, but because they worked together more closely and seamlessly.[253]

Good luck

The tips and recommendations from the previous chapters have provided you with the tools you need to successfully lead different people and forge a team in which everyone feels safe.

I would like to share one more thought with you as I say goodbye: We often believe that our behavior is transparent. That it is completely clear what we want or mean. That misunderstandings are almost impossible. Unfortunately, in this, we are very much mistaken. It is rare that others can really understand us. To speak with the words of George Bernhard Shaw: "The single biggest problem in communication is the illusion that it has taken place".

This makes it all the more important to be open, to ask questions, to assume that I may be misunderstood or misunderstand others. This is especially true if they are different from me in some important characteristics. That is why presupposing positive intentions is one of the most important rules in dealing with each other.

I wish you all the best for the future. I hope you use the tips and tricks provided here in order to act fairly as you lead others. To level differences, to do justice to different people and to achieve extraordinary results with your team.

I would also be grateful if you were to tell me about your challenges and experiences. And one final request: The whole book is about blind spots – stereotypes that influence our thinking and prejudices that we are not aware of. That also applies to me, of course. If you stumble over something to which I was blind, please let me know.

Veronika Hucke
D&I Strategy and Solutions
fair.leadership@di-strategy.com
www.di-strategy.com

Thank you

I truly enjoyed writing this book, and not just because I want to contribute to more people having fun at work. It was also an opportunity, to remember people that matter to me and colleagues who have supported me during my career, who have helped me learn and grow – and to say "thank you"!

Without Felix Rudloff, my agent at Copywrite, it wouldn't have happened. Together, we thought about what a book needs to look like that is more accessible and more fun than the regular textbook, thus reaching a broader audience. In discussions with Stephanie Walter at Campus Verlag, a comprehensive concept was developed from those initial ideas. I hope both of them enjoy the outcome as much as I do.

While writing, Lisa Kepinski was a constant companion and sparring partner, not just because of her professional experience. As an American living with her Polish husband Pawel in rural Germany, she has her own surprising everyday experiences with group dynamics.

As an employee, I have had many good bosses, but two were exceptional. I have already mentioned my first boss, Michael Krug at HP. For this book, Gottfried Dutiné was even more important. I worked with him at both Alcatel and Philips, and he supported my career as a sponsor. He also read *Fair Leadership* while I was writing it and provided me with invaluable criticism, tips and feedback.

I have lived in Germany, the US, the UK and the Netherlands and have worked in teams with colleagues from all around the world. I loved doing so. One of the highlights is my friendship with Sabrina Ma and the unforgettable road trip that took us through Central China. Also, together with our friend Liz Brady, based in New York, we experience at first hand the Bermuda Triangle-like situation of connecting across rather incompatible time zones.

One of my most impressive encounters was with my colleague Ingrid. She was the first to openly share about her experience as a transgender woman and gave me a lot of food for thought.

My unshakable certitude that women support each other, is grounded in my time at HP, working with Barbara Wollny, Eleonore Körner, Heidi Brösamle and Marion Schmidt. They offered psychological safety at its best and the most frank and unsparing feedback you can imagine. Barbara also supported my writing and together with my friend Julia Catz and Jochen Zieke has provided great insights and comments; and finally Reavis Hilz-Ward was kind enough to help finalize the English edition under great time pressure.

Without Stephanie and Manfred Confurius, *Fair Leadership* would probably still be in the making. They picked me up when I had writers' block, took me out in Hamburg and distracted me with great discussions, good food and extremely nice wine.

My sister Christina is also an indispensable source of support. Additionally, she has created the beautiful executive summary of this book.

Thank you everyone. Great to know you!

Glossary

Anchor effect: We are influenced in our judgment by the first information we receive (anchor), even if it is irrelevant. The anchor point thus becomes the reference point for our decisions. Retailers, for example, take advantage of this when giving discounts during sales or when offering products for x.99. The number before the decimal point acts as an anchor and suggests a cheaper price than the rounded amount.

Confirmation bias: The fact that people actively seek or preferentially notice information that matches their assumptions and fail to verify information that could challenge their assumptions.

Conformity: This is the public commitment to the opinion of the majority without actually sharing it.

Conformity pressure: This term refers to the pressure to seamlessly fit into a group or to support its decisions.

Descriptive gender stereotypes: They influence our perception of what women or men are supposed to be like.

Dunning-Kruger effect: People with little competence do not recognize their incompetence. They tend to overestimate their own abilities and not recognize the competence of others. The overestimation of one's own abilities is higher in the case of weak performance than in the case of strong performance.

Framing: The term stands for the presentation of information or its embedding in a certain context. This frame influences our perception. Typical example: the glass that is seen as either half full or half empty.

Gender stereotypes: The term refers to ideas and expectations as to which characteristics and behavior people of a gender typically demonstrate or that they exhibit. They are strongly influenced by culture.

Groupthink: Groupthink arises when the desire for consensus dominates or even becomes more important than solving a task well. Maintaining cohesion – unity and sense of togetherness – and solidarity in the group is more important than dealing with facts and reality.

Halo Effect: The term stands for a distortion of our perception in which single impressions have such a great radiance that they falsify our image of a person or situation. Such an effect can influence our judgement both positively (halo effect) and negatively (horn effect). As a result, we deduce from our known information other aspects that are not related.

Heuristics: These are rules of thumb that help us to come to a decision quickly and without great effort. This can lead to misjudgements and wrong decisions.

Homophiliy (social): he term refers to the tendency to surround oneself with people who are similar – for example in terms of origin, educational level or social status.

In-group and out-group: In-group is the term used by social psychologists to describe the group to which we belong due to personal relationships or demographic characteristics. The out-group consists of people with which we have less in common, feel less connected or from whom we differentiate ourselves.

Mentoring: Mentoring involves being a sparring partner, discussing professional challenges and possible strategies.

Meritocracy paradox: Scientific studies show that unequal treatment is often particularly pronounced in organizations that state that fairness is one of their core values. Because it is assumed that everyone is treated fairly, these organizations fail to check whether and where deviations actually exist and deny the need for measures that could create equal opportunities. As a result, organizations fail to take action where people are treated unfairly or experience discrimination because of personal characteristics – for example due to stereotypes or unconscious prejudices – or have different requirements.

Micro-affirmations: These are – often unconscious – signs that signal good will and support to a person, such as nodding in agreement or smiling.

Micro-inequities/Micro-aggressions: Micro-inequities are negative messages that we send to others through our behavior, facial expressions, or gestures, and that signal low esteem. The signals are subtle. The sender is often not even aware of his behavior. This does not mean that the consequences for the receiver are any less negative. In the longer term, they lose self-confidence, motivation and fun at work.

Out-group derogation: This refers to the tendency to judge the members of an out-group more critically than people with whom we have a lot in common (in-group).

Out-group (homogeneity) bias: This refers to the tendency to perceive members of a foreign group as similar and to regard characteristics or behaviors of one member as typical for all.

Out-Group: See in-group and out-group

Prescriptive gender stereotypes: They influence our view of how women or men should be.

Priming: It influences the processing of a stimulus through the activation of associations.

Privileges: In this context, privileges are advantages that a person enjoys in a particular situation due to demographics or personal background rather than any particular accomplishment. Because the situation is natural for them, people are often unaware of its effects.

Psychological safety: It means that all members of a group are convinced that it is safe to take interpersonal risks. They can show their own vulnerability without fear of negative effects on relationships, image, position or career. People feel accepted and respected with all their attributes. Psychological safety is a prerequisite for teams to perform at their best.

Sensemaking: The term describes the process by which people develop an image or a perception from available information, i.e. making sense of something. The result differs based on one's own view of the world and previous experiences.

Stereotypes: These are assumptions about the characteristics of the members of a group. They influence what we look for, how we interpret information, and what we remember. They form the basis for prejudices. There are both descriptive and prescriptive stereotypes. They influence our view of how people of a particular group are or should be and behave.

Sponsoring: In sponsoring, a manager actively supports the professional advancement of a person, for example by creating visibility, giving them access to their own network, or by bringing someone into conversation. Sponsorship – unlike mentoring – has a measurable influence on a person's career.

Unconscious bias: These are unconscious belief, thought patterns or prejudices. They can be positive or negative associations. They are so deeply rooted that they are activated without us wanting or being aware of it, or able to control it. Nevertheless, they influence our perception and judgement and lead us to make decisions that are not consistent with our conscious beliefs and values.

Bibliography

Bohnet, Iris: *What Works – Gender Equality by Design*, The Belknap Press of Harvard University Press, Cambridge, MA, 2016.

Coyle, Daniel: *The Culture Code*, Bantam Books, 2018, New York

Eddo-Lodge, Reni: *Why I am no longer talking to white people about race*, Bloomsbury, 2017, London.

Fosslien, Liz and Mollie West Duffy: *No Hard Feelings: Emotions at work (and how they help us succeed)*, Penguin Business, 2019, Great Britain

Gawande, Atul: *The Checklist Manifesto: How to get things right*, Picador, 2010, New York.

Grant, Adam: *Give and Take*, Weidenfeld & Nicolson, 2014, London.

Grant Halvorson, Heidi: *No one understands you and what to do about it*, Harvard Business Review Press, 2015, Boston

Grant Halvorson, Heidi: *9 Things successful people do*, Harvard Business School Publishing Corporation, 2012, Boston

Hewlett, Sylvia Ann, Ripa Rashid and Laura Sherbin: *Disrupt Bias, Drive Value: A New Path Toward Diverse, Engaged, and Fulfilled Talent, Center for Talent Innovation*, Rare Bird Books, 2017, Los Angeles

Kandola, Binna: *Racism at Work: The Danger of Indifference*, Pearn Kandola Publishing, 2018, Oxford

Kandola, Binna and Jo Kandola: *The Invention of Difference – The Story of Gender Bias at Work*, Pearn Kandola Publishing, 2013, Oxford

Loehken, Sylvia: *The Power of Personality: How Introverts and Extroverts Can Combine to Amazing Effect*, John Murray Learning, London, 2016

Meyer, Erin: *The Culture Map – Decoding How People Think, Lead, and Get Things Done Across Cultures*, PublicAffairs, New York, 2014.

Nielsen, Tinna and Kepinski, Lisa: *Inclusion Nudges Guide Book*, CreateSpace Independent Publishing Platform, 2016

O'Connor, Cailin and James Owen Weatherall, *The Misinformation Age*, Yale University Press, 2019

Schein, Edgar H. and Peter Schein: *Humble Leadership: The Power of Relationships, Openness and Trust*, Berrett-Koehler Publishers, 2018, Oakland

Sow, Noah: *Deutschland Schwarz Weiss*, BoD, 2018, Norderstedt

Stepper, John: *Working out Loud: For a better Career and Life*, Ikigai Press, New York, 2015

Stone, Douglas, Bruce Patton and Sheila Heen: *Difficult Conversations – How to discuss what matters most*, Penguin Books, 2010, London.

Yoshino, Kenji: *Covering – The Hidden Assault on our Civil Rights*, Random House, New York, 2007

Notes

1. "State of the American Manager, Analytics and Advice For Leaders", Gallup, 2015
2. "The Relationship Between Transformational Leadership and Followers' Perceptions of Fairness", 26.09.2012 https://link.springer.com/article/10.1007 Prozent2Fs10551-012-1507-z#page-1
3. Claudia Goldin, Cecilia Rouse, "Orchestrating Impartiality: The Impact of 'Blind' Auditions on Female Musicians", January 1997, https://www.nber.org/papers/w5903
4. "Diskriminierung am Ausbildungsmarkt, Ausmaß, Ursachen und Handlungsperspektiven", Sachverständigenrat deutscher Stiftungen für Integration und Migration, March 2014, https://www.svr-migration.de/publikationen/diskriminierung-am-ausbildungsmarkt/
5. Doris Weichselbaumer, "Discrimination against Female Migrants Wearing Headscarves", September 2016, http://ftp.iza.org/dp10217.pdf
6. Prof. Dr. Dominic Frohn, Florian Meinhold, Christina Schmidt, "Prout at work, Out im Office?!", 2017, https://www.proutatwork.de/wp-content/uploads/2018/06/PAW_ExecutiveSummary_deutsch.pdf
7. Raymond Trau, Jane O'Leary, Cathy Brown, "Myths About Coming Out at Work", *HBR*, 19.10.2018, https://hbr.org/2018/10/7-myths-about-coming-out-at-work
8. The Columbia Universität experiment is based on the Heidi Roizen case study, Kathleen L. McGinn, Nicole Tempest, Harvard Business School Case Collection, January 2000, revised ii April 2010, http://www.hbs.edu/faculty/Pages/item.aspx?num=26880
9. Iris Bohnet, *What Works*, 2016, The Belknap Press of Harvard University Press, Cambridge, MA, 2016
10. Corinne A. Moss-Racusin, Julie E. Phelan, Laurie Rudman, "When Men

Break the Gender Rules: Status Incongruity and Backlash Against Modest Men", April 2010, https://www.researchgate.net/publication/232464622_When_Men_Break_the_Gender_Rules_Status_Incongruity_and_Backlash_Against_Modest_Men

11 A. T. Kearney, 361°-Familienstudie "Mehr Aufbegehren. Mehr Vereinbarkeit!", October 2016, https://www.atkearney.de/documents/6645533/9249916/A.T.+Kearney+Familienstudie+2016.pdf/976ce5c8-0bb8-4d62-9090-59a1633dbc81

12 Australian Human Rights Commission, "Supporting Working Parents: Pregnancy and Return to Work, National Review Report", 2014

13 Derald Wing Sue, Christina M. Capodilupo, Gina C. Torino, Jennifer M. Bucceri, Aisha M. B. Holder, Kevin L. Nadal, and Marta Esquilin, "Racial Microaggressions in Everyday Life: Implications for Clinical Practice", *American Psychologist*, 05/06 2007, https://world-trust.org/wp-content/uploads/2011/05/7-Racial-Microaggressions-in-Everyday-Life.pdf

14 Ferda Ataman, "Der ethnische Ordnungsfimmel", *Spiegel Online*, 23.02.2019 http://www.spiegel.de/kultur/gesellschaft/herkunft-und-die-frage-wo-kommst-du-her-ethnischer-ordnungsfimmel-a-1254602.html

15 Original text: "Das Interessante an der Szene: Das kleine Mädchen kapiert gar nicht, worauf der Mann hinauswill. Hier prallen zwei Welten aufeinander, die nicht nur mit 60 Jahren Altersunterschied erklärt werden können. Offenbar hat die kleine Melissa, so heißt das Mädchen, ihre Karriere als 'Deutsch-Asiatin' noch nicht angetreten. Das Kind dachte bis zu dieser Begegnung doch tatsächlich, es sei aus Herne und von hier. Leider wird ihr im Laufe ihres Lebens wohl noch öfter klargemacht, dass das nicht so sei."

16 Loehken, Sylvia: The Power of Personality: How Introverts and Extroverts Can Combine to Amazing Effect, John Murray Learning, London, 2016

17 Kim Parker, Nikki Graf and Ruth Igielnik, Generation Z Looks a Lot Like Millennials on Key Social and Political Issues, Pew research Institute, 17.01.2019, https://www.pewsocialtrends.org/2019/01/17/generation-z-looks-a-lot-like-millennials-on-key-social-and-political-issues/

18 BVerfG, Beschluss des Ersten Senats, 10.10. 2017 - 1 BvR 2019/16 – Rn. (1–69)

19 Sam Killermannn, "A Guide to Gender", itspronouncedmetrosexual.com

20 Alan Garnham et al., "Gender Representation in Different Languages and Grammatical Marking on Pronouns: When Beauticians, Musicians, and Mechanics Remain Men", 2008, https://www.researchgate.net/publication/232747375_Gender_Representation_in_Different_Languages_and_Grammatical_Marking_on_Pronouns_When_Beauticians_Musicians_and_Mechanics_Remain_Men and Anatol Stefanowitsch, "Frauen natürlich ausgenommen", 14.12.2011, http://www.sprachlog.de/2011/12/14/frauen-natuerlich-ausgenommen/

21 Press release, "Automechanikerinnen und Automechaniker – Geschlechtergerechte Sprache beeinflusst kindliche Wahrnehmung von Berufen", Deutsche Gesellschaft für Psychologie, 09.06.2015, https://www.dgps.de/index.php?id=143&tx_ttnews[tt_news]=1610&cHash=1308c97486a0f55bc30d6a7cf12bf49f

22 Lin Bian, Sarah-Jane Leslie, Andrei Cimpian, "Gender stereotypes about intellectual ability emerge early and influence children's interests", *Science*, 27.01.2017, http://science.sciencemag.org/content/355/6323/389

23 Christoph Drösser, "Wo ist der Witz?", 26.07.2007, https://www.zeit.de/2007/31/Humorforschung

24 Piotr Pluta, "Different people, different ways of using humor – the Humor Styles Questionnaire", 24.10.2013, http://www.psychologyofhumor.com/2013/10/24/different-people-different-ways-of-using-humor-the-humor-styles-questionnaire-2/

25 Daniel Coyle, *The Culture Code*, Bantam Books, 2018, New York

26 Original text: "Man sollte nicht alles raushauen, was einem in den Sinn kommt. …[Es gibt] einen ausgesprochenen Hang zur Political Correctness, einschließlich strenger Regeln, wie man gender-gerecht zu sprechen hat. Das führt zu einer Verengung gesellschaftlicher Diskussionen."

27 Hannah Suppa and Torsten Gellner, "Wir haben einen ausgeprägten Hang zur Political Correctness", *Märkische Allgemeine*, 12.02.2019, http://www.maz-online.de/Brandenburg/Altbischof-Wolfgang-Huber-im-Interview-Wir-haben-einen-ausgepraegten-Hang-zur-Political-Correctness

28 Richard Wike, "Americans more tolerant of offensive speech than others in the world", Pew Research Center, 12.10.2016, http://www.pewresearch.org/fact-tank/2016/10/12/americans-more-tolerant-of-offensive-speech-than-others-in-the-world/

29   Kenji Yoshino and Christie Smith, *Uncovering talent: A new model of inclusion*, Deloitte LLP: Deloitte University. 2013

30   Randstad Arbeitsbarometer Q2, 2018, "Junge Vorgesetzte kämpfen um Akzeptanz", 06.07.2018, https://www.randstad.de/ueber-randstad/news/20180706/junge-fuehrungskraefte-kaempfen-um-akzeptanz

31   Age UK, "A Snapshot of Ageism in the UK and across Europe", March 2011, http://www.ageuk.org.uk/Documents/EN-GB/ID10180 Prozent20Snapshot Prozent20of Prozent20Ageism Prozent20in Prozent20Europe.pdf?dtrk=true

32   Thomas W. H. Ng, Daniel C. Feldman, "Evaluating Six Common Stereotypes About Older Workers with Meta-Analytical Data", 23.08.2012, https://onlinelibrary.wiley.com/doi/abs/10.1111/peps.12003

33   Stanimira Taneva, John Arnold, "Older Workers Need to Stop Believing Stereotypes About Themselves", 20.06.2016, https://hbr.org/2016/06/older-workers-need-to-stop-believing-stereotypes-about-themselve

34   Avivah Wittenberg-Cox, "Linking Gender and Generational Balance: Careers in the Age of Longevity", Forbes, 29.06.2019, https://www.forbes.com/sites/avivahwittenbergcox/2019/06/29/linking-gender-generational-balance-careers-in-the-age-of-longevity/#6fd09a841f1d

35   Lisa M. Finkelstein, Eden B. King, Elora C. Voyles, "Age Metastereotyping and Cross-Age Workplace Interactions: A Meta View of Age Stereotypes at Work", 30.12.2014, https://academic.oup.com/workar/article-abstract/1/1/26/1661637?redirectedFrom=fulltext

36   Henry Tajfel and John C. Turner, "The Social Identity Theory of Intergroup Behavior", *Psychology Press,* 2004, New York

37   Henry Tajfel, "Social Psychology of Intergroup Relations", *Annual Review of Psychology,* 1982

38   Autorengruppe Bildungsberichterstattung, Bildung in Deutschland 2018, https://www.bildungsbericht.de/de/bildungsberichte-seit-2006/bildungsbericht-2018/pdf-bildungsbericht-2018/bildungsbericht-2018.pdf

39   Universität Bremen, "Die Wohnung ist leider schon weg, Frau Gülbeyaz", 22.02.2019, https://www.uni-bremen.de/de/universitaet/presse/aktuelle-meldungen/detailansicht/news/detail/News/die-wohnung-ist-leider-

schon-weg-frau-guelbeyaz/

40 DOJ/Countrywide Settlement Information: Justice Department Reaches $335 Million Settlement to Resolve Allegations of Lending Discrimination by Countrywide Financial Corporation, The United States Attorney's Office, Central District of California, 22.06.2015, https://www.justice.gov/usao-cdca/dojcountrywide-settlement-information

41 Ten graphics on the Bechdel test, https://www.reddit.com/r/dataisbeautiful/comments/1hn1l3/ten_graphics_on_the_bechdel_test_oc/, Zugegriffen am 04.03.2019

42 Walt Hickey, "The Dollar-And-Cents Case Against Hollywood's Exclusion of Women", 01.04.2014, https://fivethirtyeight.com/features/the-dollar-and-cents-case-against-hollywoods-exclusion-of-women/?utm_content=buffered986&utm_medium=social&utm_source=plus.google.com&utm_campaign=buffer

43 Caroline Criado-Perez, *Invisible Women, Exposing Data Bias in a World Designed for Men,* Chatto & Windus, London, 2019

44 Clara Hellner, "Männer sind halt keine Patientinnen", *Zeit Online*, 25.02.2019, https://www.zeit.de/wissen/gesundheit/2019-02/gendermedizin-gesundheit-aerzte-patient-medikamente-maenner-frauen-gleichberechtigung

45 Miller McPherson, Lynn Smith-Lovin, James M Cook, "Birds of a Feather: Homophily in Social Networks", 2001, http://aris.ss.uci.edu/~lin/52.pdf

46 Herminia Ibarra, "5 Misconceptions About Networking", 18.04.2016, https://herminiaibarra.com/5-misconceptions-about-networking/

47 Center for Talent Innovation. 2013. "Innovation, diversity and market growth", September 2013

48 Mark Granovetter, "The Strength of Weak Ties", *American Journal of Sociology*, 1973, https://sociology.stanford.edu/sites/g/files/sbiybj9501/f/publications/the_strength_of_weak_ties_and_exch_w-gans.pdf

49 Jeffrey Travers and Stanley Milgram, "An Experimental Study of the Small World Problem", American Sociological Association, December 1969, https://www.jstor.org/stable/2786545?seq=1#page_scan_tab_contents

50 Herminia Ibarra, "How to Revive a Tired Network", Harvard Business Review, 03.02.2015 https://hbr.org/2015/02/how-to-revive-a-tired-network

51 Ibid.

52 Keith Ferrazzi, *Never eat alone*, Doubleday, New York, 2005

53 John Stepper, *Working out Loud: For a better Career and Life*, Ikigai Press, New York, 2015

54 John A. Bargh, Mark Chen, and Lara Burrows, "Automaticity of Social Behavior: Direct Effects of Trait Construct and Stereotype Activation on Action", *Journal of Personality and Social Psychology*, 1996, https://acmelab.yale.edu/sites/default/files/1996_automaticity_of_social_behavior.pdf

55 Thomas Mussweiler: "Doing Is for Thinking! Stereotype Activation by Stereotypic Movements", *Psychological Science,* 17, 2006

56 Kirsten Weir, "The pain of social rejection", American Psychological Association, April 2012, http://apa.org/monitor/2012/04/rejection.aspx

57 Lioba Werth, *Psychologie für die Wirtschaft*. Spektrum Akademischer Verlag, Heidelberg, 2010

58 Katherine W. Phillips et al., "Better decisions through diversity", Kellogg School of Management at Northwestern University, 01.10.2010. http://insight.kellogg.northwestern.edu/article/better_decisions_through_diversity

59 "The Mix that Matters, Innovation through Diversity", The Boston Consulting Group, April 2017

60 Max Nathan Neil Lee, "Cultural Diversity, Innovation, and Entrepreneurship: Firm-level Evidence from London", 22.10.2015, https://www.tandfonline.com/doi/abs/10.1111/ecge.12016

61 "Innovation, Diversity and Market Growth", Center for Talent Innovation, September 2013

62 Christoph Rottwilm, "So können Anleger mit Gleichberechtigung Geld machen", *Manager Magazin,* 02.04.2019, https://www.manager-magazin.de/finanzen/boerse/diversity-dax-geplant-deutsche-boerse-will-gleichberechtigung-foerdern-a-1260808.html

63 Julia Dawson, Richard Kersley, Stefano Natella, "The CS Gender 3000: The Reward for Change", Credit Suisse Research Institute, 2016

64 "Gender Diversity and Corporate Performance", Credit Suisse Research Institute, 2012, https://publications.credit-suisse.com/tasks/render/file/index.cfm?fileid=88EC32A9-83E8-EB92-9D5A40FF69E66808

65 Samuel R. Sommers, "On Racial Diversity and Group Decision Making: Identifying Multiple Effects of Racial Composition on Jury Deliberations", *Journal of Personality and Social Psychology*, 2006, http://www.apa.org/pubs/journals/releases/psp-904597.pdf

66 Joan C. Williams and Marina Multhaup, "For Women and Minorities to Get Ahead, Managers Must Assign Work Fairly", 05.03.2018, , https://hbr.org/2018/03/for-women-and-minorities-to-get-ahead-managers-must-assign-work-fairly

67 Ian Tucker, Susan Cain, "Society has a cultural bias towards extroverts", *The Guardian*, 01.04.2012, https://www.theguardian.com/technology/2012/apr/01/susan-cain-extrovert-introvert-interview

68 Sylvia Loehken, *The Power of Personality: How Introverts and Extroverts Can Combine to Amazing Effect*, John Murray Learning, London, 2016

69 Brandon Rigoni and Bailey Nelson, "For Millennials, Is Job-Hopping Inevitable?", 08.11.2016, https://news.gallup.com/businessjournal/197234/millennials-job-hopping-inevitable.aspx?utm_source=alert&utm_medium=email&utm_content=morelink&utm_campaign=syndication

70 Madeline E. Heilman, "Gender stereotypes and workplace bias", *Research in Organzational Behavior*, 2012, communal

71 J. L. Berdahl and J. A. Min, "Prescriptive stereotypes and workplace consequences for East Asians in North America", 2012, https://www.ncbi.nlm.nih.gov/pubmed/22506817

72 Linda Babcock, Maria P. Recalde, Lise Vesterlund and Laurie Weingart, "Gender Differences in Accepting and Receiving Requests for Tasks with Low Promotability", American Economic Association, 03.03.2017, https://www.aeaweb.org/articles?id=10.1257/aer.20141734

73 Madeline E. Heilman and Julie J. Chen, "Same Behavior, Different Consequences: Reactions to Men's and Women's Altruistic Citizenship Behavior", *APA PsycNet*, 2005, https://psycnet.apa.org/

record/2005-05102-002

74 Joan C. Williams und Marina Multhaup, "For Women and Minorities to Get Ahead, Managers Must Assign Work Fairly", *Harvard Business Review*, 05.03.2018, https://hbr.org/2018/03/for-women-and-minorities-to-get-ahead-managers-must-assign-work-fairly

75 Shelley Correll and Lori Mackenzie, "To Succeed in Tech, Women Need More Visibility", *Harvard Business Review*, 13.09.2016, https://hbr.org/2016/09/to-succeed-in-tech-women-need-more-visibility

76 Nancy M. Carter, Christine Cilva, "The Myth of the Ideal Worker: Does Doing All the Right Things Really Get Women Ahead?" *Catalyst*, 2011, http://www.catalyst.org/system/files/The_Myth_of_the_Ideal_Worker_Does_Doing_All_the_Right_Things_Really_Get_Women_Ahead.pdf

77 Amy Gallo, "Why Aren't You Delegating?" *Harvard Business Review*, 26.07.2012, https://hbr.org/2012/07/why-arent-you-delegating

78 Sydney Finkelstein, "Why a One-Size-Fits-All Approach to Employee Development Doesn't Work", *Harvard Business Review*, 05.03.2019, https://hbr.org/2019/03/why-a-one-size-fits-all-approach-to-employee-development-doesnt-work

79 Sam Lloyd, "Managers Must Delegate Effectively to Develop Employees", *Society for Human Resources Management*, 2012, https://www.shrm.org/ResourcesAndTools/hr-topics/organizational-and-employee-development/Pages/DelegateEffectively.aspx

80 Heidi K. Gardner, "When Senior Managers Won't Collaborate", Harvard Business Review", March 2015, https://hbr.org/2015/03/when-senior-managers-wont-collaborate

81 Catalyst, "Inclusive Leadership: The View From Six Countries", 2014, https://www.catalyst.org/research/inclusive-leadership-the-view-from-six-countries/

82 Robb Cross, Reb Rebele and Adam Grant, "Collaborative Overload", Harvard Business Review, January/February 2016, https://hbr.org/2016/01/collaborative-overload

83 Ibid.

84 Adam Grant, *Give and Take*, Weidenfeld & Nicolson, 2014, London

85 Carolyn Gregoire, "The Giving Habits of Americans May Surprise You", 06.12.2017, https://www.huffingtonpost.com/2013/08/20/are-you-a-giver-huffpost-_n_3785215.html

86 Jana Hauschild, "Warum Frauen nur einen Bruchteil aller Straftaten begehen", *Berliner Zeitung*, 25.02.17, https://www.berliner-zeitung.de/wissen/forschung-warum-frauen-nur-einen-bruchteil-aller-straftaten-begehen-26248314

87 Renee Culinan, "In Collaborative Work Cultures, Women Carry More of the Weight", *HBR*, 24.07.2017, https://hbr.org/2018/07/in-collaborative-work-cultures-women-carry-more-of-the-weight

88 Itziar Etxebarria, "Women Feel More Guilt", *Spanish Journal of Psychology, 2010,* http://www.psyarticles.com/values/guilt.htm

89 Madeline E. Heilman and Julie J. Chen, "Same Behavior, Different Consequences: Reactions to Men's and Women's Altruistic Citizenship Behavior", New York University, 2005, https://www.uccs.edu/Documents/dcarpent/altruism.pdf

90 Samuel R. Sommers, "On Racial Diversity and Group Decision Making: Identifying Multiple Effects of Racial Composition on Jury Deliberations", *Journal of Personality and Social Psychology,* 2006, Vol. 90, No. 4

91 Sheen S. Levine and David Stark, "Diversity Makes You Brighter", *New York Times*, 09.12.2015, https://www.nytimes.com/2015/12/09/opinion/diversity-makes-you-brighter.html

92 Katherine W. Phillips, "How Diversity Makes Us Smarter", *Scientific American*, 01.10.2014, https://www.scientificamerican.com/article/how-diversity-makes-us-smarter/

93 Katherine W. Phillips, "The Biases That Punish Racially Diverse Teams", 22.02.2016, *Harvard Business Review,* https://hbr.org/2016/02/the-biases-that-punish-racially-diverse-teams

94 Peter Reuell, "When bias hurts profits", *Harvard Gazette*, 22.02.2017, https://news.harvard.edu/gazette/story/2017/02/when-bias-hurts-profits/

95 Sylvia Loehken, *The Power of Personality: How Introverts and Extroverts Can Combine to Amazing Effect,* John Murray Learning, London, 2016

96 Douglas Stone, Bruce Patton and Sheila Heen, *Difficult Conversations: How to discuss what matters most,* Penguin Books, 2010, London

97 Institut für Arbeitsmarkt und Berufsforschung (IAB) der Bundesagentur für Arbeit, IAB-Kurzbericht Nr. 18, 22.8.2017, http://doku.iab.de/kurzber/2017/kb1817.pdf

98 "The Behavioural Insights Team, Promoting diversity in the Police", 24.07.2015, https://www.bi.team/blogs/behavioural-insights-and-home-affairs/

99 Kieran Snyder, "Language in your job post predicts the gender of your hire", 21.06.2016, https://textio.ai/gendered-language-in-your-job-post-predicts-the-gender-of-the-person-youll-hire-cd150452407d

100 Danielle Gaucher, Justin Friesen, Aaron C. Kay, "Evidence That Gendered Wording in Job Advertisements Exists and Sustains Gender Inequality", *Journal of Personality and Social Psychology*, Januar 2011, http://gap.hks.harvard.edu/evidence-gendered-wording-job-advertisements-exists-and-sustains-gender-inequality

101 Tara Mohr, "Why Women Don't Apply for Jobs Unless They're 100 % Qualified", *Harvard Business Review,* August 25, 2014, https://hbr.org/2014/08/why-women-dont-apply-for-jobs-unless-theyre-100-qualified

102 Alexander W. Watts, "Why Does John get the STEM Job Rather Than Jennifer?", 02.06.2014, https://gender.stanford.edu/news-publications/gender-news/why-does-john-get-stem-job-rather-jennifer

103 Binna Kandola, *Racism at Work*, Pearn Kandola Publishing, 2018

104 Marianne Bertrand and Sendhil Mullainathan, "Are Emily and Greg More Employable than Lakisha and Jamal? A Field Experiment on Labor Market Discrimination", *The American Economic Review*, 10/2004.

105 Meike Bonefeld und Oliver Dickhäuser, "(Biased) Grading of Students' Performance: Students' Names, Performance Level, and Implicit Attitudes", *Frontiers in Psychology*, 09.05.2018, https://www.frontiersin.org/articles/10.3389/fpsyg.2018.00481/full

106 Astrid Kaiser and Julia Kube, "Ungleiche Bildungschancen schon durch Vornamen? – Studie zu Vorurteilen und Vorannahmen von Lehrern", Carl von Ossietzky-Universität Oldenburg, 16.09.2009, https://idw-online.de/de/news333970

107 Amory Burchard, "Kevin ist kein Name, sondern eine Diagnose",

Tagesspiegel, 18.09.2009, https://www.tagesspiegel.de/wissen/studie-kevin-ist-kein-name-sondern-eine-diagnose/1601654.html

108 Robert Rosenthal and Lenore Jacobson, "Teachers' Expectancies: Determinants Of Pupils' IQ Gains", *Psychological Reports*, 1966, http://homepages.gac.edu/~jwotton2/PSY225/rosenthal.pdf

109 Ute Utech, Rufname und soziale Herkunft, Studien zur schichtenspezifischen Vornamenvergabe in Deutschland, Olms Verlag, Hildesheim, 2011

110 OECD (2018), *A Broken Social Elevator? How to Promote Social Mobility*, OECD Publishing, Paris

111 Lauren A. Rivera, "Guess Who Doesn't Fit In at Work", *The New York Times*, 30.05.2015, https://www.nytimes.com/2015/05/31/opinion/sunday/guess-who-doesnt-fit-in-at-work.html

112 Lauren Rivera and András Tilcsik, "Class Advantage, Commitment Penalty: The Gendered Effect of Social Class Signals in an Elite Labor Market", October 12, 2016, http://jce.sagepub.com/content/42/3/291.abstract" \t "_blank

113 Oliver Wright, "Don't wear brown shoes if you want to walk into City job", 01.09.2016, https://www.thetimes.co.uk/article/dont-wear-brown-shoes-if-you-want-to-walk-into-city-job-gfcvt2ql2

114 Jacquie D. Vorauer, Stephanie-Danielle Claude, "Perceived Versus Actual Transparency of Goals in Negotiation", 01.04.1998, https://journals.sagepub.com/doi/abs/10.1177/0146167298244004

115 Frank J. Bernieri, Miron Zuckerman, Richard Koestner and Robert Rosenthal, "Measuring Person Perception Accuracy: Another Look at Self-Other Agreement", *SAGE Journals*, Volumen 20, Ausgabe 4, 01.08.1994

116 Lauren Human, Jeremy Biesanz, "Targeting the Good Target", *Personality and Social Psychology Review*, 08/2013

117 Veronika Hucke and Lisa Kepinski, "Achieving Results: Diversity & Inclusion Actions With Impact", *Newsweek Vantage*, 2017

118 Jeffrey Dastin, "Amazon scraps secret AI recruiting tool that showed bias against women", Reuters, 10.10.2018, https://www.reuters.com/article/

us-amazon-com-jobs-automation-insight-idUSKCN1MK08G

119 Joy Buolamwini, "When the Robot Doesn't See Dark Skin", *New York Times*, 21.06.2018, https://www.nytimes.com/2018/06/21/opinion/facial-analysis-technology-bias.html

120 Candice Powell, Cynthia Demetriou, Annice Fisher, "Micro-affirmations in Academic Advising: Small Acts, Big Impact", 30.10.2013, *The Mentor, an academic advising journal*, https://dus.psu.edu/mentor/2013/10/839/9

121 Jason Dana, Robyn Dawes, Nathanial Peterson, "Belief in the unstructured interview: The persistence of an illusion, Judgment and Decision Making", September 2013, http://journal.sjdm.org/12/121130a/jdm121130a.pdf

122 Lauren A. Rivera, "Hiring as Cultural Matching: The Case of Elite Professional Service Firms", American Sociological Review, November 28, 2012, https://journals.sagepub.com/doi/10.1177/0003122412463213

123 Iris Bohnet, *What Works – Gender Equality by Design*, The Belknap Press of Harvard University Press, Cambridge, MA, 2016

124 Lauren A. Rivera, "Guess Who Doesn't Fit In at Work", *The New York Times*, 30.05.2015, https://www.nytimes.com/2015/05/31/opinion/sunday/guess-who-doesnt-fit-in-at-work.html

125 Iris Bohnet, Alexandra van Geen and Max Bazerman, "When Performance Trumps Gender Bias: Joint vs. Separate Evaluation", Management Science, 29.09.2015, https://pubsonline.informs.org/doi/abs/10.1287/mnsc.2015.2186?journalCode=mnsc" Prozent20\t

126 Timothy A. Judge and Daniel M. Cable, "The Effect of Physical Height on Workplace Success and Income: Preliminary Test of a Theoretical Model", *Journal of Applied Psychology*, 2004

127 Timothy M. Frayling et al., "Height, body mass index, and socioeconomic status: Mendelian randomization study in UK Biobank, US National Library of Medicine, National Institutes of Health, 2016, https://www.ncbi.nlm.nih.gov/pmc/articles/PMC4783516/

128 Timothy A. Judge and Daniel M. Cable. 2011. "When it comes to pay, do the thin win? The effect of weight on pay for men and women", *Journal of Applied Psychology*, January 2011, https://www.ncbi.nlm.nih.gov/pubmed/20853946

129 Francesca Righetti and Catrin Finkenauer, "If You Are Able to Control Yourself, I Will Trust You: The Role of Perceived Self-Control in Interpersonal Trust", *Journal of Personality and Social Psychology*, February 2011, https://www.researchgate.net/publication/49834955_If_You_Are_Able_to_Control_Yourself_I_Will_Trust_You_The_Role_of_Perceived_Self-Control_in_Interpersonal_Trust

130 Katherine Harmon, "Earlier model of human brain's energy usage underestimated its Efficiency", *Scientific American*, 10.09.2009, https://www.scientificamerican.com/article/brain-energy-efficiency/

131 David Rock, *Your brain at work*, New York, HarperBusiness, 2009

132 Timothy D. Wilson, *Strangers to Ourselves*, Cambridge, MA, Harvard University Press, 2004

133 Caroline Webb, *How to have a good day*, London, Crown Business, 2016

134 Daniel Kahneman, *Thinking, fast and slow*, London, Penguin Books, 2011

135 John Ridley Stroop, "Studies of interference in serial verbal reactions", *Journal of Experimental Psychology*, 1935

136 Sylvia Ann Hewlett, Ripa Rashid and Laura Sherbin, Disrupt Bias, Drive Value: A New Path Toward Diverse, Engaged, and Fulfilled Talent, Center for Talent Innovation, Los Angeles, Rare Bird Books, 2017

137 Emilio J. Castilla, "Gender, Race, and Meritocracy in Organizational Careers", *American Journal of Sociology*, Mai 2008, https://www.jstor.org/stable/10.1086/588738?seq=1#page_scan_tab_contents

138 Eric Luis Uhlmann, Geoffrey L.Cohen, "'I think it, therefore it's true': Effects of self-perceived objectivity on hiring discrimination", *Organizational Behavior and Human Decision Processes*, November 2007, https://www.sciencedirect.com/science/article/pii/S0749597807000611

139 Katie Baldiga Coffman, "Gender Differences in Willingness to Guess", *Management Science*, 2013, https://sites.google.com/site/kbaldigacoffman/research

140 Lauren A. Rivera, András Tilcsik, "Scaling Down Inequality: Rating Scales, Gender Bias, and the Architecture of Evaluation", *American Sociological Review*, 12.03.2019, https://journals.sagepub.com/stoken/default+domain/10.1177 percent2F0003122419833601-free/full

141 Buster Benson, "Cognitive bias cheat sheet, simplified", 07.01.2017, https://

medium.com/thinking-is-hard/4-conundrums-of-intelligence-2ab78d90740f

142 Matt Scott, "Top 10 Difficult Conversations: New (Surprising) Research", 29.07.2015, Chartered Management Institute, https://www.managers.org.uk/insights/news/2015/july/the-10-most-difficult-conversations-new-surprising-research

143 Sheila Heen and Douglas Stone, "Find the Coaching in Criticism", *Harvard Business Review*, 01/02, 2014

144 Binna Kandola, *Racism at Work*, Pearn Kandola Publishing, 2018, Oxford; Sylvia Ann Hewlett and Tai Green, *Black Women: ready to lead*, CTI, 2015

145 Sylvia Ann Hewlett, Noni Allwood, Karen Sumberg & Sandra Scharf with Christina Fargnoli, *Cracking the Code: Executive Presence and Multicultural Professionals*, CTI, 2013

146 *Women in the Workplace*, McKinsey and LeanIn, 2016

147 Paola Cecchi-Dimeglio, "How Gender Bias Corrupts Performance Reviews, and What to Do About It", 12.4.2017, https://hbr.org/2017/04/how-gender-bias-corrupts-performance-reviews-and-what-to-do-about-it

148 Kieran Snyder, "The abrasiveness trap: High-achieving men and women are described differently in reviews", 26.8.2014, http://fortune.com/2014/08/26/performance-review-gender-bias/

149 Shelley Correll and Caroline Simard, "Vague Feedback Is Holding Women Back", 29.04.2016, https://hbr.org/2016/04/research-vague-feedback-is-holding-women-back

150 W. C. Howell und E. A. Fleishman, *Human Performance and Productivity*. Vol 2: Information Processing and Decision Making. Hillsdale New Jersey, 1982

151 Heidi Grant Halvorson, *9 things successful people do,* Harvard Business Review Press, 2012, Boston

152 Daniel Coyle, The Culture Code: *The Secrets of Highly Successful Groups*, Bantam, 2018, New York

153 Marcus Buckingham und Ashley Goodall, "The Feedback Fallcy", *Harvard Business Review*, 03/04 2019

154 Ibid.

155 Edgar H. Schein und Peter A. Schein, *Humble Leadership: The Power of Relationships, Openness, and Trust*, Berrett-Koehler Publishers, 2018, Oakland

156 Angela Lee Duckworth & all, "Self-regulation strategies improve self-discipline in adolescents: benefits of mental contrasting and implementation intentions", *Educational Psychology*, 3/2011

157 Daniel Coyle, *The Culture Code,* New York, Bantam Books, 2018

158 Thomas J. Allen und Gunther Henn, The Organization and Architecture of Innovation: Managing the flow of Technology, Routledge, New York, Taylor & Francis Group, 2007

159 "Why You Should Rotate Office Seating Assignments", *Harvard Business Review,* 03/04, 2018

160 Nicholas Bloom, James Liang, John Roberts, Zhichun Jenny Ying, "Does working from home work?", National Bureau Of Economic Research, March 2013, https://www.nber.org/papers/w18871.pdf

161 2018 Global State of Remote Work, OwlLabs, https://www.owllabs.com/state-of-remote-work

162 Joseph Vandello, Vanessa Hettinger, Jennifer Bosson and Jasmine Siddiqi, "When Equal Isn't Really Equal: The Masculine Dilemma of Seeking Work Flexibility", Journal of Social Issues, June 2013, https://www.researchgate.net/publication/259740823_When_Equal_Isn't_Really_Equal_The_Masculine_Dilemma_of_Seeking_Work_Flexibility

163 Alternative Workplace Strategies, Fifth Biennial Global Benchmarking Study 2018, June 2018

164 Latest Telecommuting Statistics, Global Workplace Analytics, Stand 07/2018, https://globalworkplaceanalytics.com/telecommuting-statistics

165 Nicholas Bloom et al., Ibid.

166 Adam Hickman und Ryan Pendell, The End of the Traditional Manager, Gallup, Business Journal, May 31, 2018, https://www.gallup.com/workplace/235811/end-traditional-manager.aspx?

167 Lisa Kepinski and Veronika Hucke, Creating Belonging and Equity Wherever Work Takes Place, October 2019

168 Ibid.

169 Heidi Grant Halvorson, Ibid.

170 Geert Hofstede, Gert Jan Hofstede and Michael Minkov, *Cultures and organizations: Software of the mind*, Mc Graw Hill, 2010.

171 Veronika Hucke, *Mit Vielfalt und Fairness zum Erfolg*, Wiesbaden, Springer Gabler, 2017

172 Ernest Gundling und Anita Zanchettin, *Aperian Global, Global Diversity: Winning Customers and Engaging Employees within Markets*, Nicholas Brealey International, 2007

173 Erin Meyer, *The Culture Map,* New York, Public Affairs, 2014

174 Fons Trompenaars, Charles Hampden-Turner, *Riding the Waves of Culture*, Nicholas Brealey Publishing, 1997

175 Sylvia Loehken, The Power of Personality: How Introverts and Extroverts Can Combine to Amazing Effect, London, John Murray Learning, 2016

176 Adapted from von https://external-preview.redd.it/u895OhFuhxzZ9zozB-bpeTAoS4cc2JyImVaRm9YTulmA.jpg?auto=webp&s=828b5e3e2ef-c282f0bdf3b77651ebeff20c2640d

177 Jolanta Aritz, Robyn C. Walker, "Leadership Styles in Multicultural Groups: Americans and East Asians Working Together", International Journal of Business Communication, 29.01.2014, https://journals.sagepub.com/doi/abs/10.1177/2329488413516211

178 "Gen Y and the world of work: A report into the workplace needs, attitudes and aspirations of Gen Y China", Hays, 2013.

179 Erin Meyer, "Being the Boss in Brussels, Boston and Beijing", *Harvard Business Review*, 07/08, 2017

180 Joan C. Williams, Amy J. C. Cuddy, "Will Working Mothers Take Your Company to Court?" *Harvard Business Review*, September 2012

181 A. T. Kearney, "361°-Familienstudie 'Mehr Aufbegehren. Mehr Vereinbarkeit!'", Oktober 2016

182 Joseph A. Vandello, Vanessa E. Hettinger, Jennifer K. Bosson, Jasmine Siddiqi, "When Equal Isn't Really Equal: The Masculine Dilemma of Seeking Work Flexibility", Journal of Social Issues, June 2013, http://

psychology.usf.edu/faculty/data/jvandello/seekingworkflexibility.pdf

183 Yvonne Lott, "Weniger Arbeit, mehr Freizeit? Wofür Mütter und Väter flexible Arbeitsarrangements nutzen", WSI, March 2019

184 Amy J. C. Cuddy, Susan T. Fiske and Peter Glick, "Warmth and Competence as Universal Dimensions of Social Perception: The Stereotype Content Model and the BIAS Map", *Advances in Experimental Social Psychology*, Volume 40, 2008

185 Amy J. C. Cuddy, Susan T. Fiske, Peter Glick, "When Professionals Become Mothers, Warmth Doesn't Cut the Ice", *Journal of Social Issues*, Vol. 60, No. 4, 2004

186 Amy J. C. Cuddy, Susan T. Fiske and Peter Glick, "Warmth and Competence as Universal Dimensions of Social Perception: The Stereotype Content Model and the BIAS Map", *Advances in Experimental Social Psychology*, Volume 40, 2008

187 David G. Smith, Judith E. Rosenstein, Margaret C. Nikolov, "The Different Words We Use to Describe Male and Female Leaders", *Harvard Business Review*, 25.05.2018, https://hbr.org/2018/05/the-different-words-we-use-to-describe-male-and-female-leaders

188 Marianne Cooper, "For Women Leaders, Likability and Success Hardly Go Hand-in-Hand", *Harvard Business Review*, 30.04.2013, https://hbr.org/2013/04/for-women-leaders-likability-a

189 Wei Zheng, Ronit Kark and Alyson Meister, "How Women Manage the Gendered Norms of Leadership", *Harvard Business Review*, 28.11.2018, https://hbr.org/2018/11/how-women-manage-the-gendered-norms-of-leadership

190 Heidi Grant Halvorson, *No one understands you and what to do about it*, Harvard Business Review Press, 2015, Boston

191 Amy J. C. Cuddy, Matthew Kohut and John Neffinger, "Connect, Then Lead", *Harvard Business Review*, 07/08 2013

192 Amy J. C. Cuddy, Susan T. Fiske, Peter Glick and Jun Xu, "A Model of (often mixed) stereotype content: competence and warmth respectively follow from perceived status and competition", *Journal of Personality and Social Psychology*, Vol. 82, 2002

193 Amy J. C. Cuddy, Susan T. Fiske and Peter Glick, "Warmth and Compe-

tence as Universal Dimensions of Social Perception: The Stereotype Content Model and the BIAS Map", *Advances in Experimental Social Psychology*, Volume 40, 2008

194 Aaron D. Hill, Tessa Recendes, Jason W. Ridge, "Second-order effects of CEO characteristics: How rivals' perceptions of CEOs as submissive and provocative precipitate competitive attacks", *Strategic Management Journal*, May 2019, https://onlinelibrary.wiley.com/doi/10.1002/smj.2986

195 Amy J. C. Cuddy, Susan T. Fiske and Peter Glick, "Warmth and Competence as Universal Dimensions of Social Perception: The Stereotype Content Model and the BIAS Map", *Advances in Experimental Social Psychology*, Volume 40, 2008

196 Jack Zenger, "The Unlikable Leader: 7 Ways To Improve Employee/Boss Relationships", *Forbes*, 13.07.2013, https://www.forbes.com/sites/jackzenger/2013/06/13/the-unlikable-leader-7-ways-to-improve-employeeboss-relationships/#2115947f1da6, Accessed on 10.04.2019

197 Deborah Tannen, *Talking from 9 to 5: How Women's and Men's Conversational Styles Affect Who Gets Heard, Who Gets Credit, and What Gets Done at Work*, 1994, William Morrow and Company, New York

198 Alison Wood Brooks, Hengchen Dai and Maurice E. Schweitzer, "I'm Sorry About the Rain! Superfluous Apologies Demonstrate Empathic Concern and Increase Trust", *Social Psychological and Personality Science* 5, 2013

199 Nikhil Swaminathan, "Gender Jabber: Do Women Talk More than Men?", *Scientific American*, 06.07.2007, https://www.scientificamerican.com/article/women-talk-more-than-men/

200 Victoria L. Bresccoll, "Who Takes the Floor and Why: Gender, Power, and Volubility in Organizations", 29.02.2012, https://journals.sagepub.com/doi/abs/10.1177/0001839212439994

201 Elizabeth Sommers and Sandra Lawrence, "Women's ways of talking in teacher-directed and student-directed peer response groups", *Linguistics and Education*, 1992, https://www.sciencedirect.com/science/article/pii/089858989290018R

202 Shelley Correll and Caroline Simard, "Vague Feedback Is Holding Women Back", 29.04.2016, https://hbr.org/2016/04/research-vague-feed-

back-is-holding-women-back

203 LeanIn.Org and McKinsey & Company, "Women in the workplace 2016"

204 Deborah Tannen, "The Truth About How Much Women Talk — and Whether Men Listen", *Time*, 28.06.2017, http://time.com/4837536/do-women-really-talk-more/

205 Madeline E. Heilman and Michelle C. Hayes, "No Credit Where Credit Is Due: Attributional Rationalization of Women's Success in Male-Female Teams," *Journal of Applied Psychology* 90, no. 5 (2005): 905–26; http://gap.hks.harvard.edu/no-credit-where-credit-due-attributional-rationalization-women's-success-male-female-teams

206 Melissa Thomas-Hunt, Katherine W. Phillips, "When What You Know Is Not Enough", 01.05.2007, KelloggInsight, https://insight.kellogg.northwestern.edu/article/when_what_you_know_is_not_enough

207 Ernesto Reuben, Pedro Rey-Biel, Paola Sapienza and Luigi Zingales, "The Emergence of Male Leadership in Competitive Environments", IZA Discussion Paper, November 2010

208 Katherine B. Coffman, Clio Bryant Flikkema, Olga Shurchkov, "Gender Stereotypes in Deliberation and Team Decisions", Harvard Business School Working Papers, 2019, https://www.hbs.edu/faculty/Pages/item.aspx?num=55539

209 Melissa Thomas-Hunt, Katherine W. Phillips, Ibid.

210 Jennifer L. Glass et al., "What's So Special about STEM? A Comparison of Women's Retention in STEM and Professional Occupations", Oxford University Press, 21.08.2013

211 Herminia Ibarra, Nancy M. Carter und Christine Silva, "Why Men Still Get More Promotions Than Women", *Harvard Business Review*, September 2010

212 Paola Cecchi-Dimeglio, "How Gender Bias Corrupts Performance Reviews, and What to Do About It", *HBR*, 12.04.2017, https://hbr.org/2017/04/how-gender-bias-corrupts-performance-reviews-and-what-to-do-about-it

213 "Bias Interrupters: small steps, big change, Identifying & Interrupting Bias in Performance Evaluations", Center for WorkLife Law, 2016

214 Eric Luis Uhlmann, Geoffrey L. Cohen, "Constructed Criteria: Redefining Merit to Justify Discrimination", *Psychological Science*, 01.06.2005, https://journals.sagepub.com/doi/abs/10.1111/j.0956-7976.2005.01559.x?journalCode=pssa

215 Malcolm Gay, "BSO flutist settles equal-pay lawsuit with orchestra", *Boston Globe*, 14.02.2019, https://www.bostonglobe.com/arts/music/2019/02/14/bso-flutist-settles-equal-pay-lawsuit-with-orchestra/0iRyJCdjtu1BLWCAoqfQDL/story.html

216 Gardiner Morse, "Designing a Bias-Free Organization", *Harvard Business Review*, 07/08 2016

217 Sabina Nawaz, "How to Create Executive Team Norms — and Make Them Stick", *HBR*, 15.01.2018, https://hbr.org/2018/01/how-to-create-executive-team-norms-and-make-them-stick

218 Atul Gawande, *The Checklist Manifesto: How to get things right*, Picador, 2010, New York

219 Exploring the Color of Glass: Letters of Recommendation for Female and Male Medical Faculty: https://journals.sagepub.com/doi/abs/10.1177/0957926503014002277

220 Atul Gawande, *The Checklist Manifesto: How to get things right*, Picador, 2010, New York

221 Amy Langfield, "'Queen Bee' stereotype in the workplace is a rarity", 08.03.2013, https://www.today.com/money/queen-bee-stereotype-workplace-rarity-1C8768020.

222 Olga Khazan, "Why Do Women Bully Each Other at Work?", *The Atlantic*, September 2017, https://www.theatlantic.com/magazine/archive/2017/09/the-queen-bee-in-the-corner-office/534213/

223 Belle Derks and Naomi Ellemers, "Do sexist organizational cultures create the Queen Bee?", *British Journal of Social Psychology*, 25.03.2011, https://onlinelibrary.wiley.com/doi/abs/10.1348/014466610X525280

224 Michelle Duguid, "Female tokens in high-prestige work groups: Catalysts or inhibitors of group diversification?", *Organizational Behavior and Human Decision Processes*, September 20122, https://source.wustl.edu/2012/05/women-dont-advocate-for-other-women-in-highstatus-work-groups/

225 Ibid.

226 Cristian L. Dezső, David Gaddis Ross, Jose Uribe, "Is there an implicit quota on women in top management? A large-sample statistical analysis", Wiley Online Library, 15.11.2015, https://onlinelibrary.wiley.com/doi/abs/10.1002/smj.2461

227 "Die Macht hinter den Kulissen: Warum Aufsichtsräte keine Frauen in die Vorstände bringen", Allbright Stiftung, April 2019

228 Sarah Dinolfo, Christine Silva, Nancy M. Carter, "High Potentials in the pipeline: Leaders pay it forward", Catalyst, 2012

229 Olga Khazan, op. cit.

230 Allen, Tammy D., "Rewarding Good Citizens: The Relationship Between Citizenship Behavior, Gender, and Organizational Rewards" (2006). *Psychology Faculty Publications.* 28, https://scholarcommons.usf.edu/psy_facpub/28

231 Laurie A. Rudman, Peter Glick, "Prescriptive Gender Stereotypes and Backlash Toward Agentic Women", *Journal of Social Issues*, Vol. 57, No. 4, 2001, https://wesfiles.wesleyan.edu/courses/PSYC-309-clwilkins/week4/Rudman.Glick.2001.pdf

232 Elisabeth Kelan, Linchpin – Men, Middle Managers and Gender Inclusive Leadership, Cranfield University 2015

233 Aarti Ramaswami, George F. Dreher, Robert Bretz and Carolyn Wiethoff, "Gender, mentoring, and career success: the importance of organizational context", *Personnel Psychology*, 12.05.2010

234 Sylvia Ann Hewlett, "The Real Benefit of Finding a Sponsor", *HBR*, 26.01.2011, https://hbr.org/2011/01/the-real-benefit-of-finding-a

235 Catalyst, "Coaches, mentors, and sponsors – Understanding the differences", 11.12.2014, https://www.catalyst.org/wp-content/uploads/2019/01/understanding_coaches_mentors_sponsors.pdf

236 Center for Talent Innovation, "The Sponsorship Dividend", 2019, https://www.talentinnovation.org/_private/assets/TheSponsorDividend_Key-FindingsCombined-CTI.pdf

237 Sylvia Ann Hewlett, "Mentors Are Good. Sponsors Are Better", *New York Times*, 13.03.2013

238 Sylvia Ann Hewlett, "As a Leader, Create a Culture of Sponsorship", *HBR*, 08.10.2013, https://hbr.org/2013/10/as-a-leader-create-a-culture-of-sponsorship

239 David Smith and Brad Johnson, "When Men Mentor Women", *HBR* Webinar, 23.10.2018, https://hbr.org/ideacast/2018/10/when-men-mentor-women.html

240 Sylvia Ann Hewlett, "Smart Leaders Have Protégés", *HBR*, 09.08.2013, https://hbr.org/2013/08/smart-leaders-have-proteges

241 David Smith and Brad Johnson, "When Men Mentor Women", *HBR* Webinar, 23.10.2018, https://hbr.org/ideacast/2018/10/when-men-mentor-women.html

242 W. Brad Johnson and David G. Smith, "Mentoring Women Is Not About Trying to 'Rescue' Them", *Harvard Business Review*, 14.03.2018, https://hbr.org/2018/03/mentoring-women-is-not-about-trying-to-rescue-them, Wendy Murphy, "Advice for Men Who Are Nervous About Mentoring Women", *Harvard Business Review*, 15.03.2019, https://hbr.org/2019/03/advice-for-men-who-are-nervous-about-mentoring-women

243 Emilia Bunea, Svetlana N. Khapova and Evgenia I. Lysova, "Out of Office", *Harvard Business Manager*, May 2019

244 Jake Herway, "How to Create a Culture of Psychological Safety", Gallup, 07.12.2017, https://www.gallup.com/workplace/236198/create-culture-psychological-safety.aspx?g_source=link_wwwv9&g_campaign=item_247799&g_medium=copy

245 Jane Smith, "What to Do if You're Surrounded by Yes-People", Gallup, 15.03.2019, https://www.gallup.com/workplace/247799/surrounded-yes-people.aspx

246 Cailin O'Connor and James Owen Weatherall, *The Misinformation Age*, Yale University Press, 2019

247 "Cultural Diversity at Work: The Effects of Diversity Perspectives on Work Group Processes and Outcomes", 01.06.2001

248 Catalyst, "Inclusive Leadership: The View From Six Countries", 2014

249 A. W. Woolley, C. F. Chabris, , A. Pentland, N. Hashmi, N. & T. W. Malone, "Evidence for a collective intelligence factor in the performance

of human groups", *Science*, 330(6004), 686-688, 2010, http://www.cs.cmu.
edu/~ab/Salon/research/Woolley_et_al_Science_2010-2.pdf

250 Amy Edmondson, "Psychological Safety and Learning Behavior in Work Teams", *Administrative Science Quarterly*, Vol. 44, No. 2, June 1999

251 Kathleen M. Eisenhardt, Jean L. Kahwajy, L. J. Bourgeois III, "How Management Teams Can Have a Good Fight", *HBR*, July/August 1997, https://hbr.org/1997/07/how-management-teams-can-have-a-good-fight

252 Juliet Bourke, *Which Two Heads Are Better Than One?: How diverse teams create breakthrough ideas and make smarter decisions*, Australian Institute of Company Directors, 2016

253 Daniel Coyle, *The Culture Code*, Bantam Books, 2018, New York and Peter Skillman, "Marshmallow Design Challenge", Youtube, https://www.youtube.com/watch?v=1p5sBzMtB3Q

Printed in Great Britain
by Amazon